VELCRO GOD

Wyatt & Sons Publishers books may be ordered through booksellers or by contacting:

Wyatt & Sons Publishers, LLC
Mobile, Alabama 36695
www.wyattpublishing.com
editor@wyattpublishing.com

Because of the dynamic nature of the Internet, any web address or links contained in this book may have changed since publication and may no longer be valid.

Cover design by:Bubba Crowder
Interior design by: Mark Wyatt
ISBN 13:978-1-954798-21-2
Printed in the United States of America

VELCRO GOD

RELATING TO THE GOD OF ATTACHMENT

by
MATT DAY

WS

WYATT & SONS
PUBLISHERS, LLC

Mobile, AL◆ www.wyattpublishing.com

DEDICATION

To the Body of Christ, that they might know Him
and the power of His resurrection.

CONTENTS

Introduction:

The God of Attachment

I've been thinking a lot about Velcro in relationship to God—hence the name *"Velcro God."*

Velcro, in my opinion, is a cool invention. It's used all over the world in many different products like shoes, board shorts, and wallets. NASA really made Velcro popular by using it on their space suits. [1]

It works by using a hook and loop system that is patterned after some things found in creation like sand spurs and burrs. As with Velcro, when the tiny hooks are pressed to the tiny loops, it sticks. Because of its uniqueness, the guy who invented it was inducted into the National Inventors Hall of Fame in 1999. [2]

God is a lot like Velcro in relationship to us, because the God we serve is a God of attachment. Let me explain. When God created the world, He did not do so because He was lonely. He did not do so because He was bored or because needed someone to interact with. To characterize God in that way would, in effect, be saying that God is in some way lacking. Not only would this be an inaccurate understanding of God, but it would also be Biblical heresy.

"The God who made the world and everything in it is the Lord of heaven and earth and does not live in temples built by human hands. [25]

*And he is not served by human hands, **as if he needed anything**. Rather, he himself gives everyone life and breath and everything else"* (Acts 17:24-25 NLT, emphasis mine).

This is not what I mean when I say that God is attached. God is not lacking in anything. He is totally fulfilled in Himself and is in need of no one or nothing. The attachment of God to which I am referring is this:

It is how God has chosen to work in and relate to the world that He created.

J. I. Packer's book, *Knowing God*, has really impacted my understanding about this highly important concept. In his chapter on *"The Love of God,"* he makes a statement that has helped to develop my understanding of who God is and how He has decided to work in relationship to His creation.

*"We have in previous chapters made the point that God's end in all things is his own glory—that he should be manifested, known, admired, adored. This statement is true, but it is incomplete. It needs to be balanced by a recognition that through setting his love on human beings God has **voluntarily bound up his own final happiness with theirs.** It is not for nothing that the Bible habitually speaks of God as the loving Father and Husband of his people. It follows from the very nature of these relationships that **God's happiness will not be complete till all his beloved ones are finally out of trouble**...God was happy without humans before they were made; he would have continued happy had he simply destroyed them after they had sinned; but as it is he has set his love upon particular sinners, and this means that by his own free voluntary choice, **he will not know perfect and unmixed happiness again till he has brought every one of them to heaven. He has in effect resolved that henceforth for all eternity his happiness shall be conditional upon ours.**"* [3]

The last line of the quote says, *"He (God) has in effect resolved that henceforth for all eternity his* (God's) *happiness shall be conditional upon ours."* Let this sink in for one second. Our powerful, great, awesome God has voluntarily bound up His eternal happiness with His creation. When we sin, He grieves. When we repent, He rejoices, and you see this all throughout Scripture.

Please don't ask me why God has chosen to do this. The only reason I can think of is that it brilliantly shows how intimate and personal God is as He relates to His creation, but nonetheless, isn't this an intriguing thought? The idea of God being bound or attached to His creation. It started me thinking about how *else* God has bound Himself up, or attached Himself, to his creation. For instance, consider this equation.

If you do...

Then I will...

If you don't do...

Then I will...

It's an equation that is found all throughout Scripture. Look at what God said to Solomon after Solomon dedicated the Temple:

*"As for you, **if you will** follow me with integrity and godliness, as David your father did, obeying all my commands, decrees, and regulations, ⁵ **then I will** establish the throne of your dynasty over Israel forever. For I made this promise to your father, David: 'One of your descendants will always sit on the throne of Israel.' ⁶ "**But if you** or your descendants abandon me and disobey the commands and decrees I have given you, and if you serve and worship other gods, ⁷ **then I will** uproot Israel from this land that I have given them. **I will** reject this Temple that I have made holy to honor my name. **I will** make Israel an object of mockery and ridicule among the nations"* (1 Kings 9:4-7, NLT, emphasis mine).

Did you catch it? *If you will...then I will. If you do not...then I will have no other choice but to do this.* Can you see the attachment of God in these verses? His actions are attached to our decisions, and the pattern is found all over Scripture.

Here is the Biblical understanding of the attachment of God, and this is the point of the entire book.

When we attach ourselves to the things to which God has attached Himself, we find God and the blessings of God. Conversely, when we avoid these things, we avoid God and His blessings.

Let me give you two broad, overarching things to help our understanding of how God has chosen to work in the world that He created that will serve as the backdrop for this entire book.

God works with His creation, not above it.

Author Philip Yancey talks about this in one of his books. He writes:

"...from the very beginning, God has relied on human partners to advance the process of creation. After equipping Adam to cultivate the land and supervise the animals, God left the work of the garden in his hands. All through history, the pattern has continued...When God wanted a dwelling place on earth, a tabernacle and a temple did not descend from the sky like a spaceship; thousands of artists and craftsmen worked to fashion them...God has made the work of the kingdom **dependent** *on the notoriously unreliable human species."* 4

When my children were smaller, it was much easier for me to work on something alone, without their help. I could work so much faster. I didn't have to stop and undo what had been done *"wrong,"* or worry about any little fingers or toes getting hurt. I'm sure the same thought process can be ascribed to God, choosing to work alone or with His creation, but God has chosen to take the path of working with His creation and through His creation even though it is a slow, messy process. Remember the story of Jonah?

God called Jonah to go to Nineveh to announce His judgment upon the city, and Jonah takes off in the opposite direction. God doesn't then say, *"Oh well, I guess I will have to do it Myself."* No, He pursues Jonah, His chosen instrument, to deliver His message. Jonah surrenders, but not until he was in the belly of a whale. Talk about being stubborn!

Here's the point. God loves to work with His creation, and this is the way God has set the world to work. He, just as Phillip Yancey described, *"has made the work of the kingdom dependent upon the notoriously unreliable human species."*

Let me give you the second understanding of God when it comes to attachment:

God is a corporate God

What do I mean? God has primarily attached Himself to the community, not necessarily the individual. Is salvation an individual thing? Yes. Is God personal to each one of us? Yes, but how He relates to us is primarily through the community as a whole. Look at the following examples:

*"Do not take any of the things set apart for destruction, or you yourselves will be completely destroyed, and you will bring trouble **on the camp of Israel.** [19] Everything made from silver, gold, bronze, or iron is sacred to the LORD and must be brought into his treasury"* (Joshua 6:18-19, NLT, emphasis mine).

What's happening in these verses? Israel is about to defeat mighty Jericho. They had been marching and praying around the seemingly impenetrable wall for several days, doing exactly what the Lord commanded. Right before the wall fell, God called them together and gave them specific instructions. *"When the walls fall, don't take anything from Jericho that is set apart for destruction."* Clear enough. *"If anyone does, that person will bring trouble on the camp of Israel."*

In other words, if one person sins, everybody is punished. Israel pushes ahead, and they destroy Jericho, but look at what happens next.

*"But **Israel** violated the instructions about the things set apart for the LORD. **A man** named Achan had stolen some of these dedicated things, **so the LORD was very angry with the Israelites.** Achan was the son of Carmi, a descendant of Zimri son of Zerah, of the tribe of Judah"* (Joshua 7:1, NLT, emphasis mine).

A man, one man, named Achan, disobeyed the Lord's command, but God doesn't declare that Achan sinned, He says that *"Israel"* disobeyed Him, and that He was *"angry with the Israelites,"* not just Achan. Achan sins and yet all of Israel suffers the consequences.

In their next battle against this tiny town of Ai, the Israelites were soundly defeated. Thirty-six men were killed, and all of Israel was paralyzed with fear. It was only after Israel dealt with the sin that God started blessing them again.

Before I analyze this, let me give you another example: Remember when David ordered his officers to count the people in his kingdom?

Satan rose up against Israel and caused David to take a census of the people of Israel. ² So David said to Joab and the commanders of the army, "Take a census of all the people of Israel—from Beersheba in the south to Dan in the north—and bring me a report so I may know how many there are."

³ But Joab replied, "May the LORD increase the number of his people a hundred times over! But why, my lord the king, do you want to do this? Are they not all your servants? Why must you cause Israel to sin?"

⁴ But the king insisted that they take the census, so Joab traveled throughout all Israel to count the people. Then he returned to Jerusalem (1 Chronicles 21:1-4, NLT).

Now, there is nothing inherently wrong with counting people. I mean, God placed a whole book in the Bible and called it *"Numbers."* God had even ordered census' of Israel to be taken in the past. So, what's the big deal?

Satan tempted David with pride in himself and confidence in his numbers instead of his God, and he took it. Even his commanding officer, Joab, who was hardly a saint knew it was wrong and knew there would be consequences—*"why must you cause Israel to sin?"* David pushed ahead, the people were counted, and Israel suffered mightily for it.

*"God was very displeased with the census, and he punished **Israel** for it"* (1 Chronicles 21:7, NLT emphasis mine).

70,000 people died as a result of what David did. 70,000!

Think about God when you think about these examples. Achan sinned against God, and Israel was punished. David sinned against God, and Israel was punished. Now do you understand how big of a deal community is to God?

"But, Pastor Matt, that's not fair. This is like you having a conversation with a room full of people telling them not to go outside or there will be consequences. If one person decides to sneak out and disobey, everyone in the room gets punished?"

Let me help you understand this by giving you a different example. Think about the sin of Adam in the Garden of Eden. Did his sin only affect him? No way. His sin unleashed sin into the world so that every person born after him would have the proclivity and the propensity for sin. Every person born after Adam is born with a sin nature.

On the other hand, think about Jesus. His one act of dying on the cross, unleashed forgiveness and reconciliation to God for anyone who comes to Him in faith. The Apostle Paul describes it this way in Romans 5.

"Yes, Adam's one sin brings condemnation for everyone, but Christ's one act of righteousness brings a right relationship with God and new life for everyone. ¹⁹ Because one person disobeyed God, many became sinners. But because one other person obeyed God, many will be made righteous" (Romans 5:18-19, NLT).

When Adam sinned, sin entered the world and brought condemnation for everyone, but Christ's one act of righteousness brought about the possibility of a right relationship with God and new life for everyone.

Understand, God doesn't just deal with the individual. In God's mind, He likens us to a team sport not an individual event. Everyone on the team wins together. Everyone on the team loses together. He is a corporate God, and He deals primarily with the community.

Think about how the Church in the New Testament is described. *"The Body of Christ."* Body is an interesting word choice. Concerning your own physical body, you have one body but many parts make up that one body. These parts do not act independently of one another. You don't have the fingers on your hand and your two feet acting on their own accord. That would look really silly. When one part of your body hurts, the rest of your body hurts. In the same way, this is how God views us. He primarily views us as a whole, not as individuals.

In light of this information, how important now is your individual role within the body of Christ?

The community is something that God has attached Himself to, and this is how He has chosen to relate to humanity—on a corporate level. Do I fully understand it? Do I think that it's fair for God to work this way? Honestly? No, but I know Scripturally this is how He has chosen to work.

Back when I pastored a traditional church, I would say often to my congregation: *"If our church is healthy, but the one down the street is not, that affects us."* Why would I say that? Because I understood that God works on a corporate level. This is why we became a help to so many churches around us. If our cities are to be reached, it is the responsibility of the believers in it to work together, because God is a corporate God.

Let me close with this: If you knew for certain how God has chosen to work in and relate to this world, and if you knew the things that God has attached Himself to, wouldn't you want to figure those things out? Wouldn't you want to know these things and attach yourself to them?

Here's the deal. They are not secrets. They are straight out of the Word of God, and they are not hard to find. My prayer is that when you are done with this book, you will clearly understand what these principles are, and you will begin to truly know God, obey God, and have a greater understanding of how He has chosen to work.

---

[1] Jake Swearingen, *An Idea That Stuck: How George de Mestral Invented the Velcro Fastener*, (November, 2016). www.nymag.com.

[2] De Mestral, George. www.encyclopedia.com.

[3] J.I. Packer, *Knowing God: 20th Edition*, (InterVarsity Press, 1993), 125 (Emphasis mine).

[4] Phillip Yancey, *Prayer: Does It Make Any Difference? 1st Edition*, (Zondervan Books, 2006), 109-110.

Chapter 1

Attached To The Word

One of the reasons that I am so burdened to write this book is to help the people of God understand how God has revealed Himself in the Scriptures. From what I have observed, there is a level of mediocrity that is pervasive among Christians in the United States today that can be attributed, I believe, to a gross neglect of the Word of God. Our culture, including the Church culture, is becoming at a very rapid rate Biblically illiterate. We just don't know God's Word.

As a result of that Biblical illiteracy, many of God's people live in direct opposition to how God intends for them to live, and it's not that they are shaking their fists in open rebellion to the Lord. Many of the people that I am describing truly love God and are sincere in their hearts towards Him. They live in opposition to Him because they have failed to understand God's Word and thus, the attachment characteristic of God—who He is, where He is working, and what He has attached Himself to in relationship to the world that He has created.

They are like the people in 2 Kings 22 who lost God's Word and forgot what it said. Because God's Word was neglected and not passed down to the next generation, they lived in passive rebellion to the commands of the Law that God had given them to obey.

When the king heard what was written in the Book of the Law, he tore his clothes in despair. ¹² Then he gave these orders to Hilkiah the priest, Ahikam son of Shaphan, Acbor son of Micaiah, Shaphan the court secretary, and Asaiah the king's personal adviser: ¹³ "Go to the Temple and speak to the Lord for me and for the people and for all Judah. Inquire about the words written in this scroll that has been found. For the Lord's great anger is burning against us because our ancestors have not obeyed the words in this scroll. We have not been doing everything it says we must do" (2 Kings 22:11-13, NLT).

It was only when the Word of God was found that they could repent and obey the Lord. We must do the same.

While I was in pastoring in Florida, I served for a couple of seasons as the minor league spring training baseball chaplain for the Baltimore Orioles. I loved working with those young men, helping them develop into mature men of God. As I got to know them and speak to them at chapel services, I soon realized that I was involved in a worldwide ministry. Let me explain.

The players all came from various parts of the world to the organization. They would then go on to play for minor league Oriole teams that were all over the country, and they would return to their home states or countries after the season was over. It dawned on me that I wasn't dealing with something that was just local. This was global in nature. That's why I vowed to equipped those young men with the greatest thing I could give them—the ability to read the Word of God for themselves. Understand clearly. You will never grow in your relationship with God apart from the Word of God, because:

God has attached Himself to His Word

This means that you will never succeed spiritually, you will never live the abundant life that Jesus talks about, you will never experience the truest blessings from the Lord, you will never understand the will of God, the heart of God, and the mind of God apart from continually reading and obeying God's Word. Let me give you some verses to help you understand this concept.

But Jesus told him, "No! The Scriptures say, 'People do not live by bread alone, but by every word that comes from the mouth of God'" (Matthew 4:4, NLT).

Jesus says that we spiritually live by every word that comes from the mouth of God. The Word of God is our spiritual nourishment, our spiritual bread, just like physical food is our physical nourishment. What's wrong with many people today and many churches today is that they are malnourished.

A Gallup news article recently reported that less than one-quarter of the American adult population (20%) believes the Bible is the actual Word of God and is to be taken literally word for word. This is down from the last survey conducted in 2017. The article also said that the majority of those Americans who don't believe that the Bible is literally true, believe that even though it is the inspired Word of God, not everything in it should be taken literally. [1]

George Barna has done extensive research on the U.S. population concerning Biblical worldviews, which is basically believing the core, foundational truths that the Bible teaches. His research concluded that only 4% of the population has a Biblical worldview and that only 13% of those claiming to be born again hold to a Biblical worldview. [2] Do you know why these numbers are so low? Sadly, most people never bother to read the Word of God.

I love eating food fresh off the grill. Man, what a treat! What you put on the grill is sustenance—it tastes good and it satisfies. What if you were to approach your spiritual nourishment like your physical nourishment? As far as the physical goes, most of us would never even consider missing a meal! Do we approach our spiritual nourishment the same way?

My life verse from the age of 13 is still my favorite.

*"As newborn babes desire the sincere milk of the Word **so that you may grow** thereby, now that you have tasted that the Lord is good"* (1 Peter 2:2-3, NKJV, emphasis mine).

Did you catch the key phrase in that passage? *"So that you may grow."* Apart from the Word of God, you can't grow because God has attached Himself to His Word. If you neglect attaching yourself to the Word on a consistent basis,

How do you know what God's will is?

How do you know what truth is?

How do you know what God wants you to do or doesn't want you to do?

How do you know what God wants for your life?

How do you know how to find God?

How do you know how to understand God?

How do you know how to please God?

How do you know in what direction to go?

How do you know what promises from God to claim for your life?

How do you know how to manage money, what to do in marriage, how to discipline and handle your children, how to deal with the relationships in your life?

How do you know where to find encouragement, confidence, strength, boldness, peace, assurance?

You find all of these things and more in the Word of God because God has attached Himself to His Word. Just look at all of the verses that describe the Word of God.

It says it is a **Sword**

"For the word of God is alive and powerful. It is sharper than the

sharpest two-edged sword, cutting between soul and spirit, between joint and marrow. It exposes our innermost thoughts and desires" (Hebrews 4:12, NLT).

It says it is a **Mirror**

"But don't just listen to God's word. You must do what it says. Otherwise, you are only fooling yourselves. ²³ For if you listen to the word and don't obey, it is like glancing at your face in a mirror. ²⁴ You see yourself, walk away, and forget what you look like. ²⁵ But if you look carefully into the perfect law that sets you free, and if you do what it says and don't forget what you heard, then God will bless you for doing it" (James 1:22-24, NLT).

It says it is a **Hammer**

"Is it (My Word) not like a mighty hammer that smashes a rock to pieces?" (Jeremiah 23:29b, NLT, *additions mine*).

It says it is **Water**

"For husbands, this means love your wives, just as Christ loved the church. He gave up his life for her ²⁶ to make her holy and clean, washed by the cleansing of God's word" (Ephesians 5:25-26, NLT).

It says it is **Silver and Gold**

"The law from your mouth is more precious to me than thousands of pieces of silver and gold" (Psalm 119:72, NIV).

It says it is **Fire**

"Is not my word like fire," declares the LORD, (Jeremiah 23:29a, NLT).

It says it is a **Lamp**

"Your word is a lamp for my feet, a light on my path" (Psalms 119:105, NIV).

When I was younger, a popular singing group came and did a concert at my home church. Something happened that night that had a profound impact on my life. One of the guys in the group quoted Psalm 1:1-3 from memory. The experience was so meaningful that I decided to memorize that same passage that very night.

"Blessed is the man

Who does not walk in the counsel of the ungodly,
Nor stands in the way of sinners,

Nor sits in the seat of the scornful;
² But his delight is in the law of the Lord,

And in His law does he meditate day and night.
³ He shall be like a tree

Planted by the rivers of living water,

That brings forth its fruit in its season,
Whose leaf shall not wither;

And whatever he does he prospers" (Psalm 1:1-3, NKJV).

Stop and look at this passage for one second. The Psalmist says that his delight is in the Word of God. His chief desire is to know the Word of God. I believe every true believer will have a God birthed desire for the Word of God. If God lives in you and God wrote the Bible, it makes sense. In every true believer there should be a desire to read the Word, a desire to listen to the Word preached, a desire to hear the Word sung, and a desire to live out and obey the Word of God because God has attached Himself to His Word. Look again at Psalm 1.

Blessed is the one *(Oh the happiness of the one)* **who does not walk in step with the wicked or stand in the way that sin-**

ners take or sit in the company of mockers, (Psalm 1:1, NIV, *additions and italics mine*)

The book of Psalms begins with the understanding that happiness is not found in things that are in opposition to God. This person doesn't walk, stand or sit in the company of evil, those who oppose God or His ways. He doesn't delight to go with, hang out with, sit down and scheme with those who do evil. Contrarily, this man's happiness is not found in anything that goes against God or involves the pleasure of sin. Why? He's found something better.

"Blessed is the one...whose delight is in the law of the Lord and who meditates on his law day and night" (Psalm 1:1a and 2, NIV).

This man takes delight in the Word. All that makes him happy and satisfied is found in the Word of God. Knowing it, obeying it, and living by it is his chief business, highest occupation and highest delight. It is in the Law of the Lord that he finds supreme joy.

This is not referring to law in the legal sense but the totality of the revelation of God—all that is found in the Word of God. This is what the Psalmist seeks, and this is what brings him the greatest joy. Notice what he does with it.

He meditates on His law, day and night. It consumes his thinking. He reflects on it in the course of his daily activities whether it be in his family life, business life, personal life, church life, financial life, political life, or leisure life. The Word permeates every portion of His life. It is relevant to his every situation, and he thinks about it all the time.

Does this characterize your life? Does the Word of God have such pre-eminence in your life that it affects all you do? When faced with a decision, is your first thought *"What does the Bible say about that?"* It should! Look at what happens when the Word of God takes priority in a person's life.

"That person is like a tree planted by streams of water, which yields its fruit in season and whose leaf does not wither—whatever they do prospers" (Psalms 1:3, NIV).

Did you read that? The Psalmist says that the person who revolves his life around the Word of God will be like a tree; a strong, solid, mighty tree, that is planted. In other words, it is purposely placed and securely fastened.

Where is it planted? It is planted by streams of water which means that it receives constant nourishment. It yields fruit in season, meaning that it works the way it is supposed to—bearing fruit at exactly the right time. Notice also that its leaf does not wither. Not withering means that it is divinely protected as it is nourished in the ways of God.

The text closes with this statement: *"whatever they do prospers."* It mirrors the same promise found in James 1 which says, *"then God will bless you for doing it."* It means that whatever that person does, God honors it and blesses it. This is the reward for attaching our lives to the Word of God and Godly living.

How do we get to the point of making sure everything we do centers on the Word of God? Let me give you a couple of things.

Make sure the Holy Spirit is on the inside

Only a person who has Christ living on the inside, can truly understand the Word of God. This is what happens when a person cries out to God for salvation. God comes to live on the inside of that repentant sinner. In other words, the Author of Life and the Author of the Word of God has now come in to take up residence in a person's life. Notice how the Bible puts it:

"What we have received is not the spirit of the world, but the Spirit who is from God, so that we may understand what God has freely given us. [13] This is what we speak, not in words taught us by human wisdom but in words taught by the Spirit, explaining spiritual realities with Spirit-taught words. [14] The person without the Spirit does not accept the things that come from the Spirit of God but considers them foolishness, and cannot understand them because they are discerned only through the Spirit" (1 Corinthians 2:12-14, NIV; italics mine).

You cannot understand the Word of God without the Holy Spirit. He is the pass key, and if you don't have the Holy Spirit in your life, do not make that an excuse. Read the Word, and ask the Holy Spirit to make it real to you.

Make sure the Holy Spirit is happy

Once He comes to live on the inside of your life, make sure to keep Him happy. Whatever He tells you to get rid of, get rid of. Whatever He tells you to confess, confess. Whatever He tells you to obey, obey. Whatever He calls *"sin,"* call *"sin."* You do not want your relationship with Jesus to be grieved or quenched in any way.

Ephesians 4 says *"Don't grieve the Holy Spirit of God,"* and 1 Thessalonians chapter 5 says *"Don't quench the Holy Spirit."* In other words, don't do anything that would cut off or limit His power in your life, or make Him sad. That's what sin does every time. This is why I say, *"Make sure the Holy Spirit is happy."* Don't cut off and grieve the power supply that leads to understanding.

Make sure the Holy Spirit has the proper tools to work with

I believe every true believer will have a God birthed desire in them for the Word of God since God is attached to it. If God wrote the Bible, and God lives in a person, it makes sense that the person will now want to crave it. Because the devil also knows this, he will do everything he can to distract you in this spiritual battle.

Because of that fact, there has to be a time that you set aside during the day for you to get into the Word of God, hear from the Lord, and stoke that desire. Therefore, find a set time during the day to read the Bible that works for your wiring. Make sure it is the same time during the day so that a habit can form. If you are a morning person, find time in the early morning. If you are a night owl, find time when everyone goes to bed, but make it a priority. When reading, follow these simple steps:

Same Bible, Readable Bible:

If at all possible, read from the same Bible every time, and make sure your Bible is readable and understandable.

Pen In Hand:

Always read the Bible with a pen in hand. Underline what stands out to you. Write notes in your Bible. Ask questions of the texts. Write down prayers to the Lord in the margins of your Bible. Don't be afraid to mark it up. The Bible is meant to be underlined.

Quiet Place:

Find a place that is alone and unplugged from the rest of the world. Turn off your cell phone. Don't try to commune with the Lord in a room filled with noise and people. Retreat to a quiet place so that God can minister to you, and you can pour your heart out to Him. Make sure that place becomes your *"spot"* to retreat to often. Again, this is about building a familiar routine.

Good Strategy:

Here's what I do: I get to a quiet spot. I often begin my time with the Lord by singing something to Him. Worship is a great way to get into the presence of God. Next, I generally pray something like this before I read, *"Lord, speak to me as I open Your Word."*

I have a to-do list with me so that I can write down anything that I need to do that day as the Lord brings it to mind. I read at least four chapters when I read the Bible—a chapter from the Old Testament, a chapter from the New Testament, a chapter from Psalms, and a chapter from Proverbs.

I don't read randomly but strategically. I read each book of the Bible as its own book, from beginning to end. I write in the margins of my Bible or in my journal things that God is saying to me or prayers that I want God to do in me, and then I close with a time of prayer. Let me close with these two admonitions.

Be determined

Reading the Bible is not based on how you feel that particular day. Be determined to meet with God no matter what, regardless of how you feel. God will begin to transform you as you meditate on His Word. The Bible is made up of 66 books, written by 40 different authors, over a period of 1500 years, in 3 different languages, yet there are no contradictions morally, philosophically, ethically, judicially, legally or spiritually and it reads like it was written and collaborated in a back room with every writer present. They all share a common theme—the salvation that God offers freely to all people in Jesus. It is a supernatural book because it is the Word of God. Be determined to read it!

Make sure the Holy Spirit knows your desire

One of the best things you can do is pray and ask God for the desire to know His Word more. Ask Him to give you an overwhelming desire to get into His Word and delight in His Word. Don't you know that God wants to grant that in you? It's a prayer that He stands ready to answer. Ask Him to place a deep desire in you for His Word and watch Him work. He's excited to show you what's inside. God has attached Himself to His Word. Read it, attach yourself to it, and be changed because of it.

---

[1] Frank Newport, *"Fewer in U.S. Now See Bible as Literal Word of God,"* (July 6, 2022), www.news.gallup.com.

[2] Tracy Munsil, *"Biblical Worldview Among U.S. Adults Drops 33% Since Start of COVID-19 Pandemic,"* (February 28, 2023 | CRC | *American Worldview Inventory 2023* from the Cultural Research Center at Arizona Christian University), www.arizonachristian.edu.

Chapter 2

Attached To Prayer

When Paul talks about the spiritual armor in Ephesians 6 that we are to put on and appropriate, it is clear that Paul wanted prayer to be included in the description of our spiritual armor. You can hear the military language with which he uses to describe prayer—*"stay alert, be persistent..."*

The main difference between this piece of spiritual armor and the others is that Paul doesn't make it analogous to anything. There is the Belt of Truth, the Breastplate of Righteousness, the Shoes of Peace, the Shield of Faith, the Helmet of Salvation, the Sword of the Spirit...and prayer.

Prayer is such a mystical thing. What concrete object do you put with it to describe prayer? If only Paul had *Star Wars* available for him to watch. Prayer, in my opinion, is like The Force. It is the mystical, powerful, unseen, mind altering, object moving, covering, protecting weapon, available to every believer.

William Cowper, the great hymn writer, once penned these words:

Restraining prayer we cease to fight.

Prayer keeps the Christian's armor bright

And Satan trembles when he sees,

the weakest saint upon his knees.[1]

Because prayer, like The Force, has a mystical element to it, there's a lot of confusion when it comes to prayer. For example, when someone says, *"I'll pray for you,"* what is your gut reaction? *"Thank you so much"* or *"I'd rather you tangibly help me out instead?"*

Some of you might live in the land of disillusionment and hurt when it comes to prayer. Maybe you prayed and prayed about something and it didn't work out the way you hoped. *"What's the use"* just might be your philosophy now.

I once had a guy walk into my office who shared with me a glimpse of his spiritual story. He said that he was involved in a church body a few years ago. He gathered with them all the time, became a Christian, and became very active in the ministry of the church. Then, he walked away from it all. He said the reason that he walked away from the Church and God is that he had prayed and prayed for something to happen and God was silent. He became so disillusioned that he came to the conclusion that God no longer existed.

I firmly believe that there are many Jesus believing people who pray, but who at the same time are really not convinced of its importance. They struggle to understand the reason why. Why pray? I've asked myself this question many times.

When Amy and I were first married, I worked at a furniture store in Jackson, Mississippi, in order to put her through Occupational Therapy school. I had a unique job at the furniture store—the only one of its kind. My job consisted of selling furniture, assembling furniture, and delivering furniture. I could sell you a piece of furniture one day, assemble it the next, and be the one who drops it off at your house not too long after that. Now that's customer service!

When I was working in the warehouse, I remember one day talking to my delivery manager, who was a very Godly man, about prayer. The conversation went something like this: *"So, do you really think prayer works?"* Without hesitation he said to me, *"Prayer moves the hand of God."* In other words, God is attached to prayer.

I've thought about that conversation for a long time. After college and even into my time in seminary, I struggled in grasping the reason for prayer. I knew that the Bible told me to pray, and I knew from growing up in church that prayer is something you try, and do, and attempt to engage in, but for some reason I just couldn't figure out why we were to do it. The sovereignty of God always stood in my way.

Here's what I mean. If God is all sovereign and has the future mapped out, and knows what's going to happen next, why pray? I mean, who am I to change the mind and the plan of Almighty God? Can those plans even be changed? Why would God want to change them anyway? Isn't He all-knowing, and doesn't He know what is best? See what I mean? Yet, when I read my Bible, I see people praying as if praying does change the heart and hand of God, including Jesus. Have you ever examined the prayer life of Jesus?

Jesus Taught About Prayer

*"But **when you pray**, go away by yourself, shut the door behind you, and pray to your Father in private. Then your Father, who sees everything, will reward you"* (Matthew 6:6, NLT, emphasis mine).

It was not, *"if you pray"* but *"when you pray."*

*One day Jesus was praying in a certain place. When he finished, one of his disciples said to him, "Lord, teach us to pray, just as John taught his disciples." ² He said to them, "**When you pray**, say: "'Father, hallowed be your name, your kingdom come. ³ Give us each day our daily bread. ⁴ Forgive us our sins, for we also forgive everyone who sins against us. And lead us not into temptation"* (Luke 11:1-4, NIV, emphasis mine).

Again, Jesus says, *"When you pray,"* and when asked how to pray, Jesus taught them.

Jesus Engaged In Prayer

Not only did Jesus teach about prayer, Jesus prayed. Very often we see Jesus on this earth retreating and disconnecting in order to pray.

"Very early in the morning, while it was still dark, Jesus got up, left the house and went off to a solitary place, where he prayed" (Mark 1:35, NIV).

"But Jesus often withdrew to the wilderness for prayer" (Luke 5:16, NLT).

"And after he had dismissed the crowds, he went up on the mountain by himself to pray. When evening came, he was there alone" (Matthew 14:23, ESV).

Jesus Got Angry Concerning Prayer

Jesus often became angry with those around him who did not recognize the importance of prayer. For instance, remember the time Jesus cleansed the Temple and used a whip to chase everyone out? Why did He do this?

He said to them, "The Scriptures declare, 'My Temple will be called a house of prayer,' but you have turned it into a den of thieves!" (Matthew 21:13, NLT).

When Jesus and the disciples were in the synagogue, they noticed a religious leader and a lowly tax-collector praying. Jesus told them in Matthew 6,

"When you pray, don't be like the hypocrites who love to pray publicly on street corners and in the synagogues where everyone can see them. I tell you the truth, that is all the reward they will ever get. ⁶ But when you pray, go away by yourself, shut the door behind you, and pray to your Father in private. Then your Father, who sees everything, will reward you" (Matthew 6:5-6, NLT).

Jesus told His disciples not to pray like the religious leader.

When Jesus was in the Garden, agonizing with His Father about the monumental task that was set before Him, enduring the horrific suffering on the cruel cross, He previously asked his disciples to stay alert and pray. When He came back to check on them and found them asleep, He became angry.

Then Jesus went with them to the olive grove called Gethsemane, and he said, "Sit here while I go over there to pray." ³⁷ He took Peter and Zebedee's two sons, James and John, and he became anguished and distressed. ³⁸ He told them, "My soul is crushed with grief to the point of death. Stay here and keep watch with me." ³⁹ He went on a little farther and bowed with his face to the ground, praying, "My Father! If it is possible, let this cup of suffering be taken away from me. Yet I want your will to be done, not mine." ⁴⁰ Then he returned to the disciples and found them asleep. He said to Peter, "Couldn't you watch with me even one hour? ⁴¹ Keep watch and pray, so that you will not give in to temptation. For the spirit is willing, but the body is weak!" (Matthew 26:36-41, NLT).

Jesus often became angry when prayer was not happening or was being done incorrectly.

Jesus, At This Moment, Is Praying

"Who then will condemn us? No one—for Christ Jesus died for us and was raised to life for us, and he is sitting in the place of honor at God's right hand, pleading for us" (Look at Romans 8:34 (NLT).

"Therefore he is able, once and forever, to save those who come to God through him. He lives forever to intercede with God on their behalf" (Hebrews 7:25, NLT).

Jesus is interceding and praying for His chosen right now.

Now, I want you to think about prayer and think about Jesus for one second. Jesus is the Second Person of the Trinity. Jesus is God in the flesh who is all-knowing, all-seeing, ever-present, and all-powerful, and Jesus prayed while on this earth, consistently and passionately! Jesus became visibly upset when prayer was not carried out, and what is Jesus doing right now at the right hand of the throne of the Father? He is praying for you and me!

But again, my mind starts wandering as to why. Why did Jesus deem it necessary to pray? I mean He's God incarnate. He and the Father are One, and He knows the future. Jesus, in the Gospel accounts, is described as being all knowing, reading people's thoughts and answering those thoughts before they are even spoken, yet He prayed. Let that sink in. Jesus prayed and He is currently praying right now in His glorified state.

If Jesus found prayer to be vitally important, how much more important should prayer be to us? Yet, even after reading all of this, there is still much confusion about prayer because we see it as something mystical rather than something concrete, but the concrete understanding of prayer is that the God of the universe has attached Himself to it to this understanding:

When we pray, God works.

When we don't pray, He doesn't.

I have become totally convinced of this truth, and because God is attached to prayer, this is just how He has chosen to work with His creation and operate in the world that He has created.

This is why Martin Luther described his prayer life by saying,

"I have so much to do that I shall spend the first three hours in prayer." [2]

Pastor and author David Jeremiah says this about prayer:

"God has hard-wired the universe to work through prayer." [3]

The great theologian Karl Barth said this about prayer:

"To clasp the hands in prayer is the beginning of an uprising against the disorder of the world." [4]

Ask yourself this question. If you were absolutely convinced that when you prayed, God worked, and when you didn't pray, He didn't, would that cause you to pray more or pray less? You would say, *"Of course, it would cause me to pray more."*

Okay, this is how Jesus understood prayer. This is how the great men and women of God understood prayer, and this is how I want you to understand prayer. Prayer is vitally important for God being able to work in your life, your circumstances, and in someone's salvation, because it is the way that He has hardwired the world to work. He has attached Himself to prayer, and the more you are convinced of that, the more you will pray.

In the next chapter, I'm going to go a little deeper into this subject, but I want to close with a quote by the Prince of Preachers, Charles Haddon Spurgeon.

"Prayer bends omnipotence of heaven to your desire. Prayer does move the arm that moves the world" [5]

Prayer moves the hand that moves the world, and it moves the all-powerful God to action because He is attached to it. This is how God has chosen to work in the world, through the prayers of His people.

---

[1] Edwin F. Hatfield, *"The Church Hymn Book for the Worship of God"* (Ivison, Blakeman, Taylor and Company, NYC, 1872), 932.

[2] Relevant Magazine, *"18 Martin Luther Quotes That Still Ring True,"* (October 31, 2017), www.relevantmagazine.com.

[3] David Jeremiah, *"The Prayer Matrix,"* (Multnomah, 2004), back cover.

[4] Daniel L. Migliore, *"The Lord's Prayer: perspectives for reclaiming Christian prayer,* (Eerdmans, 1993), 18-19.

[5] The Spurgeon Center, *"9 Ways To Pray Like Charles Spurgeon,"* (October 27, 2016), *www.spurgeon.org.*

Chapter 3

Attached To Asking

I firmly believe that there are many Jesus believing people who pray, but who are, at the same time, not really convinced of its importance. They struggle to understand the reason why to pray. But, as we observed about prayer in the last chapter, we came to understand very clearly that God has attached Himself to it. When we pray, God works. When we don't pray, He doesn't. This is how much God has attached Himself to prayer. Notice all the times in the Scriptures that we are commanded to pray.

"Pray in the Spirit at all times and on every occasion. Stay alert and be persistent in your prayers for all believers everywhere" (Ephesians 6:18, NLT).

Pray at all times, on every occasion, for believers everywhere!

"Never stop praying" (1 Thessalonians 5:17, NLT).

Think about this: why would we be commanded to pray if prayer did not move the hand of God? I want to dive a little deeper into this subject because I believe it requires further explanation. What is it exactly about our prayers that moves God to action? I believe the answer to that is in the understanding of *"asking."*

When we ask,

God acts.

Asking unlocks the heart of God because God has attached Himself to asking. Jesus, while speaking to His disciples says in Luke 10:

These were his instructions to them: "The harvest is great, but the workers are few. So pray to the Lord who is in charge of the harvest; **ask** *him to send more workers into his fields"* (Luke 10:2, NLT, emphasis mine).

When I first analyzed this verse, I had to wrestle with a few things. If the harvest is great and the workers are few, why then doesn't the Lord of the Harvest just send more workers? Sounds simple enough. God, who is in charge of the harvest, should assess the situation and take care of it, right? I mean, doesn't He know that more workers are needed? Isn't it His responsibility to handle the situation?

But, Jesus makes it very clear that it's not enough for God to know what needs to be done. He must be asked to do it. *"Pray to the Lord who is in charge of the harvest; ASK him to send more workers into his fields."* Look at this next verse.

"Simon, Simon, Satan has asked to sift each of you like wheat. But I have pleaded in prayer for you, Simon, that your faith should not fail" (Luke 22:31-32, NLT).

Again, Jesus doesn't give Peter five steps to defeating the devil. Jesus also doesn't step in and handle the situation in His own power. Certainly, Jesus has the power to stop the enemy from sifting one of His boys. No, Jesus operates under the system that God has set up—*"I have pleaded in prayer for you that your faith should not fail."*

Look at what James, the brother of Jesus said:

"You want what you don't have, so you scheme and kill to get it. You are jealous of what others have, but you can't get it, so you fight and wage war to take it away from them. Yet you don't have what you

*want because you don't **ask** God for it"* (James 4:2-3, NLT, emphasis mine).

There it is again. According to the brother of Jesus, you do not have what you want because God is waiting on you to ask for it. Look at what Paul tells the Ephesian believers.

*"And pray for me, too. **Ask** God to give me the right words so I can boldly explain God's mysterious plan that the Good News is for Jews and Gentiles alike. ²⁰ I am in chains now, still preaching this message as God's ambassador. So pray that I will keep on speaking boldly for him, as I should"* (Ephesians 6:19-20, NLT, emphasis mine).

The Apostle Paul pleads for the Church to ask God to give him the right words. Are you picking up the theme here? God is attached to asking. There have been several moments in my life when this truth has been clearly impressed upon me.

South Florida was a strange place to me when I first arrived for my first pastorate. Let me explain. I grew up in Alabama, the deep South. Living in the South is a very unique experience, especially when it comes to *"Southern Hospitality."* It's not just a phrase, it is a way of life, at least it was when I was growing up. People were genuinely hospitable. We opened doors for each other, said *"hello"* to perfect strangers, carried on lengthy conversations with people standing in the check-out line and started another one with the cashier when it was our turn to pay. A person who kept to himself was considered rude according to southern rules of etiquette. Acknowledging people with a wave or a nod was a social standard in the South.

When the Lord called me to south Florida to pastor a church, I soon realized that I was leaving the *"deep South"* and heading into the *"deep North."* Nobody spoke with a southern accent, and every license plate I saw was from somewhere else—Michigan, Ohio, New York, New Jersey, Canada, and many others.

As I lived in this strange place, I began to notice that the people I came in contact with were not generally friendly to me. For instance, I would hold a door open to let people go through and no *"thank you"* was even offered for my kind hospitality. Other times I would look people in the eye ready to say *"hello"* or nod at them acknowledging their existence, and they never even looked my way. I was in culture shock! How could I travel ten hours below the deep South and arrive somewhere outside of the deep South?

I began to get discouraged and even cynical. I started to act differently. I stopped saying *"thank you,"* and I stopped looking people in the eye. I was miserable acting this way, but I was up for the challenge. One day, I was sitting in my vehicle telling God about my culture shock, and then it happened. The Lord pressed these words upon my heart. *"Why don't you just ask Me?"*

Ask God to make the people I meet hospitable to me? I had never thought of that before. I had such a peace that this inkling was indeed from the Lord, and I got so excited. I bowed my head and prayed, *"God, I ask that You would make the people around me hospitable towards me."* Here's what I noticed. God did not fail to answer the challenge! The people that I encountered from then on were the friendliest people. They looked me in the eye, said *"hello"* to me, and said *"Thank you"* when I opened the door for them. God did that. I asked and He answered, because God has attached Himself to asking.

A few weeks ago, I was in Park City, Utah for our Children's Hope Chest Board Retreat. As I was talking to our board president, she told me a story of how God had spoken to her. When she was around 11 years old, she developed an ovarian cyst that became very painful. She arrived at the county hospital where they took x-rays and identified the issue, but they told her they couldn't help her. She would have to drive 30 minutes to the bigger city hospital for them to do surgery.

While on the way, the pain became so intense, but then it happened. She said the Lord whispered to her these words: *"I'm here. Just ask Me."* She said to the Lord through her pain, *"Please take my pain away"* and immediately it was gone. When they got to the hospital, the staff was ready to take her in for surgery, but she bounded out of the car as if nothing was wrong. Needless to say, they didn't do the surgery, even though the previous x-rays showed that they needed to. It was no longer needed because the Lord healed her because of her simple request. *"I'm here. Just ask Me."* God is attached to our asking! Asking unlocks God working in our circumstances!

"Pastor Matt, are you actually saying that God responds to our asking, that He wants us to ask?" This is exactly what I'm saying. When we ASK, God ACTS. In Luke 11, Jesus tells an interesting story about prayer that has confused a lot of people.

One day Jesus was praying in a certain place. When he finished, one of his disciples said to him, "Lord, teach us to pray, just as John taught his disciples" (Luke 11:1, NIV).

The disciples come to Jesus asking Him to teach them to pray. Notice how Jesus responds.

Then Jesus said to them, "Suppose you have a friend, and you go to him at midnight and say, 'Friend, lend me three loaves of bread; ⁶ a friend of mine on a journey has come to me, and I have no food to offer him.' ⁷ And suppose the one inside answers, 'Don't bother me. The door is already locked, and my children and I are in bed. I can't get up and give you anything.' ⁸ I tell you, even though he will not get up and give you the bread because of friendship, yet because of your shameless audacity he will surely get up and give you as much as you need. ⁹ "So I say to you: Ask and it will be given to you; seek and you will find; knock and the door will be opened to you. ¹⁰ For everyone who asks receives; the one who seeks finds; and to the one who knocks, the door will be opened. ¹¹ "Which of you fathers, if your son asks for a fish, will give him a snake instead? ¹² Or if he asks for an egg, will give him a scorpion? ¹³ If you then, though you are evil, know how to give good gifts to your children, how much more will your Father in heaven give the Holy Spirit to those who ask him!" (Luke 11:5-13 (NIV).

What a seemingly strange story Jesus tells in this passage. Here the disciples are coming to Jesus, asking Him to teach them how to pray, and Jesus responds with a story. In this story, God likens himself to a neighbor who is in bed and doesn't want to be bothered. For a long time, this passage troubled me because I didn't understand it. In it I saw the reluctance of God. If I keep on asking, God will reluctantly give me what I want, regardless if it is his will, just to get me off his back. I saw it as me, or anybody, coming to God and bothering Him with my persistent requests.

Let me give you some background with this story that Jesus tells. During this time period, travel was done usually by night. Since it was a dry, desert climate, it made perfect sense to travel in the cool of the evening rather than in the scorching noonday sun. When this traveler arrives at his friend's house, the friend is caught unprepared—there was no bread in the house.

The owner of the house did what any logical person would have done in that time, he went on a hunt to find food. His lack of hospitality had now become everyone's problem in that community, and they were obligated to meet their neighbor's need. Well, almost everyone felt obligated.

The breadless man knocks on the door of the only unwilling participant in the village. *"Don't bother me...it's late...my family is already tucked away in bed...I don't want to get up...go away."* This guy clearly did not want to be bothered.

By the way, everyone hearing this story rolling off Jesus' tongue would have been laughing hysterically at this point. This kind of refusal to help a neighbor was comical and unheard of. In a culture heavily based on shame, you never refused your neighbor. To do so would risk bringing the entire village to your doorstep by daybreak!

The bothered man finally gets out of bed, not because he suddenly wants to be a friend to this man, and not because he understands the society of shame that he is living in, and not because he finally comes to the realization that getting up is the right thing to do. The only reason he gets up is to shut the man up who is persistently knocking on his door!

This doesn't sound very loving does it? As a matter of fact, it sounds downright rude. From this story, Jesus leaps into a discourse on persistence—ask, seek, knock. Keep on asking, keep on seeking, and keep on knocking.

What does all of this mean? I mean, how does this highlight the character of God? Let me tell you. God is not symbolic of the man in the bed. He is a contrast to the man in the bed. Here's what Jesus is trying to say. If this rude, cranky neighbor will eventually get up and give you what you want, how much more will a God who loves you and desires to give to you respond to your requests? This is the punch behind the passage because this is exactly what God is like!

It has been told that there was an officer in the city of Rome who was appointed to always have his doors open in order to hear from and receive any Roman citizen who came to him for help. [1]

God is the same way! His door is always open to the cry of anyone willing to ask. It is His highest priority to help them. Our asking is His constant delight, and Jesus proves this in the next couple of verses.

"Which of you fathers, if your son asks for a fish, will give him a snake instead? [12] Or if he asks for an egg, will give him a scorpion? [13] If you then, though you are evil, know how to give good gifts to your children, how much more will your Father in heaven give the Holy Spirit to those who ask him!" (Luke 11:11-13, NIV).

If you parents, who are evil, know how to bless your children with good things, then what about a God who is completely good? *"How much more"* is the phrase used to describe the Father. Get the idea? God is good! He is madly in love with us! He loves it when we ask Him. It is a principle in the word of God, and God works it out and comes to the rescue when we ask!

D.L. Moody, the great evangelist of the 19th century tells a story relating to the importance of asking:

There was a man in England who got up in a meeting and made one of those wonderful prayers, but there was no petition in it. And there was a poor, godly saint who could not stand it any longer, and she cried out, "Ask God for something." Now, that is just it. "Ask, and ye shall receive; knock and it shall be opened to you." That's a promise; now let's lay hold of it. [2]

But, hold on. We still have this whole sovereignty thing to deal with in prayer. God is sovereign, and God knows what we are going to ask BEFORE we ask, so where do you put the sovereignty of God in prayer? Great question. Here is the understanding of Scripture:

You place it at the end of your prayers, not at the beginning.

When we put God's sovereignty at the beginning of our prayers, we become so limited in asking God because instead of asking God, we try to figure Him out. We labor to figure out if this is His will or if this is what God wants to do. It's the very opposite of what He wants! Our job is to ask. It is His job to answer and handle the sovereignty. It is not our job to try and figure out what His answer is going to be. We must ask! Abraham Heschel, who greatly studied the Prophets in the Bible, talks about how the prophets of old prayed.

"The refusal to accept the harshness of God's ways in the name of love was an authentic form of prayer. Indeed, the ancient prophets of Israel were not in the habit of consenting to God's harsh judgment and did not simply nod, saying, 'Thy will be done.' They often challenged Him, as if to say, 'Thy will be changed'." [3]

In other words, they didn't try to figure out the will of God before they asked. They asked and then relied upon the will of God to dictate the answer. They placed sovereignty at the end of their prayers, not at the beginning.

A great example of this is when King David pleaded for his child to live. When the child was sick, he fasted and prayed and He asked for the child to live. When the child died, he got up and worshipped the Lord, and excepted His sovereign answer.

Abraham asked God to spare the cities of Sodom and Gomorrah.

Moses asked God to not destroy His own people.

Solomon asked God for wisdom.

Gideon asked God for a sign (twice!).

Jesus asked His Father to let the cup of suffering pass from Him.

Paul asked God for open doors to share the Gospel.

We, like them, can ask God for:

a hedge of protection,

wisdom,

open doors,

provision,

the ability to forgive,

God to change your marriage, your children, and we could go on and on.

Sovereignty goes at the end of our asking, when God has answered, not at the beginning. Therefore, ask first, and keep on asking. Then, rely on the sovereignty of God. Let, *"God I ask You to (fill in the blank)"* become a huge part of your prayer life, because God is attached to asking.

---

[1] D.L. Moody, *"Prevailing Prayer,"* (Moody Publishers, Chicago, 2016 ed.), 100.

[2] John W. Reed, *"1100 Illustrations from the writings of D.L. Moody: For Teachers, Preachers, and Writers,"* (Baker Pub Group, 1996), 218.

[3] Phillip Yancey, *"Prayer: Does It Make Any Difference?"* 1st Edition, (Zondervan Books, 2006), 96.

Chapter 4

Attached To Fasting

You can't legitimately talk about prayer and asking without talking about fasting. All of these go together when you talk about prayer. With that understanding, however, there is a lot of confusion about the discipline of fasting. What is it? How is it done, and most importantly for our understanding, why is it to be done?

Let me give you the definition of fasting.

"Fasting is refraining from food for a spiritual purpose."

The noun translated *"fast"* or *"fasting"* in the Hebrew and Greek languages means the voluntary abstinence from food. The literal Hebrew translation is *"not to eat."* The literal Greek means *"no food."* I can hear the questions now. *"Why would anyone want to voluntarily go without food?"* Here's the Biblical response:

God has attached Himself to fasting

Before we understand how He has done this, let's spend some time understanding fasting from the life, ministry, and teaching of Jesus.

"Then Jesus was led by the Spirit into the wilderness to be tempted there by the devil. ² For forty days and forty nights he fasted and became very hungry" (Matthew 4:1-2, NLT).

I find it very moving that Jesus fasted, that Jesus voluntarily went without food for spiritual purposes. Understand, if Jesus, God in the flesh, fasted and prayed, how much more do you think we need to fast and pray? But, not only did Jesus fast, He also expected his followers to fast. Notice the language that He uses in the following verses.

"When you give to someone in need, don't do as the hypocrites do—blowing trumpets in the synagogues and streets to call attention to their acts of charity! I tell you the truth, they have received all the reward they will ever get" (Matthew 6:2, NLT).

"When you pray, don't be like the hypocrites who love to pray publicly on street corners and in the synagogues where everyone can see them. I tell you the truth, that is all the reward they will ever get" (Matthew 6:5, NLT).

"And when you fast, don't make it obvious, as the hypocrites do, for they try to look miserable and disheveled so people will admire them for their fasting. I tell you the truth, that is the only reward they will ever get. ¹⁷But when you fast, comb your hair and wash your face" (Matthew 6:16-17, NLT).

"When you give, when you pray, and when you fast." No spiritual person would question if we are supposed to pray as followers of God. No spiritual person would question if we are supposed to financially give. Therefore, no one under the influence of the Holy Spirit should question if we are to fast. It is not an option in the Christian life, but an expectation. Look at all the people in the Bible that prayed and fasted. It's a who's who list.

"Moses remained there on the mountain with the LORD forty days and forty nights. In all that time he ate no bread and drank no water. And the LORD wrote the terms of the covenant—the Ten Commandments—on the stone tablets" (Exodus 34:28, NLT).

Moses fasted.

They said to me, "Things are not going well for those who returned to the province of Judah. They are in great trouble and disgrace. The wall of Jerusalem has been torn down, and the gates have been destroyed by fire." ⁴ When I heard this, I sat down and wept. In fact, for days I mourned, fasted, and prayed to the God of heaven (Nehemiah 1:3-4, NLT).

Nehemiah fasted when preparing to rebuild the wall.

Elijah fasted.

Daniel fasted on numerous occasions.

Ezra fasted and mourned over the state of Israel.

Esther asked Mordecai to gather the Jews and fast for her for 3 days and nights.

Samuel ordered a corporate fast for all of Israel, as did Jehoshaphat.

David fasted for his dying child to be healed.

Anna, the prophetess awaiting to see the coming of the Messiah, regularly fasted and prayed.

"Anna, a prophet, was also there in the Temple. She was the daughter of Phanuel from the tribe of Asher, and she was very old. Her husband died when they had been married only seven years.³⁷ Then she lived as a widow to the age of eighty-four. She never left the Temple but stayed there day and night, worshiping God with fasting and prayer" (Luke 2:36-37, NLT).

Paul fasted for the elders that he commissioned in every church body.

"Paul and Barnabas also appointed elders in every church. With prayer and fasting, they turned the elders over to the care of the Lord, in whom they had put their trust" (Acts 14:23, NLT).

"With prayer and fasting, they turned the elders over to the care of the Lord." The early Church, for at least 400 years after Christ, fasted twice each week. ¹

Martin Luther maintained the spiritual discipline of fasting. So did

John Calvin. [2]

Upon establishing the Methodist Church, John Wesley considered fasting to be so important that he required all candidates for ordination to fast until 3pm on Wednesdays and Fridays. [3]

Watchman Nee says this about fasting,

"Since prayer is a desiring after God, and fasting is a denying of self, faith will instantly be sparked when these two factors are joined." [4]

Bill Bright, founder of Campus Crusade, says this,

"Fasting is one of the most powerful spiritual disciplines of all the Christian disciplines...Through fasting and prayer, the Holy Spirit can transform your life," [5]

Andrew Murray says,

"Prayer needs fasting for its full and perfect development."

He also says, *"Prayer is the one hand with which we grasp the invisible; fasting, the other, with which we let loose and cast away the visible."* [6]

Wesley Duewel, in one of his sermons on fasting, says this:

"How shocked many Christians will be in heaven to see what blessings they missed and how often they failed all that God intended to do through them just because they did not add fasting to their prayer." [7]

He goes on to say in his sermon,

"Satan tries to make you hesitate to fast, to procrastinate about fasting. Why be surprised? He fears tremendously lest your prayer be empowered by fasting. He may even temporarily try to battle you all the more if you fast. He may become desperate. You are greatly endangering his work when you fast and pray." [8]

With much of the Bible focused on fasting and with so many spiritual giants dedicated to consistent fasting, it makes you ask, *"What's so important about fasting?"* Here's the answer. Yes, God has attached Himself to fasting, and the reason for this is:

Fasting, coupled with prayer, unlocks things that CANNOT otherwise be unlocked.

There are certain things that are locked up in God's economy that can only be unlocked and released when prayer is coupled with fasting. Do I understand all of this? No, but Jesus made this clear to His disciples.

And when He had come into the house, His disciples asked Him privately, "Why could we not cast it out?" ²⁹ So He said to them, "This kind can come out by nothing but prayer and fasting" (Mark 9:28-29, NKJV).

The reason the demon could not be cast out, according to Jesus, is that it required fasting to accompany prayer. Again, fasting unlocks things in God's economy that could not otherwise be unlocked. I believe this principle is true for physical healing, overcoming bondage, discerning God's specific direction for your life, spiritual renewal or breakthrough, the salvation of people, and more! The reason why we don't see more of these things happening, in my opinion, is that we have failed to see how God has attached Himself to fasting.

Let's dig a little deeper into this by asking this question: *"Who presently rules the world?"* Not too long ago, I had a strange encounter with my Bible. When I read the encounter of the devil tempting Jesus in the wilderness, something grabbed my attention.

Then the devil took him up and revealed to him all the kingdoms of the world in a moment of time. ⁶ "I will give you the glory of these kingdoms and authority over them" the devil said, "because they are mine to give to anyone I please. ⁷ I will give it all to you if you will worship me" (Luke 4:5-7, NLT).

The devil says to Jesus about the kingdoms of the world that they belong to him and that he has the authority to give them to anyone he wishes. He says this to Jesus and offers the kingdoms of the world to Jesus, the second person of the Triune God! He offers them to the One by whom all things were made and exist and have their being!

Notice what Jesus does not say to the devil. He does not say, *"Whoa, wait a minute. I am God in the flesh. I created everything you see. You can't give anything to Me because it all belongs to Me. Be gone."* He doesn't say that at all. He never corrects the devil's language. He simply says to him in verse 8:

"You must worship the Lord your God and serve only him" (Luke 4:8, NLT).

The Bible recognizes that the devil has great authority. It was given to him when Adam and Eve sinned in the garden, when sin was unleashed to humanity. That open door of sin brought with it the authority of the devil, to legally rule on this earth and in the world's system. Three times Jesus calls the devil the *"ruler of this world."*

*"The time for judging this world has come, when Satan, **the ruler of this world**, will be cast out"* (John 12:31, NLT, emphasis mine).

*"I don't have much more time to talk to you because **the ruler of this world** approaches..."* (John 14:30, NLT, emphasis mine).

*"Judgment will come because **the ruler of this world** has already been judged"* (John 16:11, NLT, emphasis mine).

The Apostle Paul, in his letter to the Corinthian Church says about the devil's authority,

*"Satan, who is **the god of this world** has blinded the minds of those who do not believe"* (2 Corinthians 4:4, NLT, emphasis mine).

Look at the language found in 1 John 5:

*"We know that we are children of God and that the world around us is **under the control of the evil one**"* (1 John 5:19, NLT, emphasis

mine).

The early Church strongly believed that they *"lived on a planet ruled by powers intent on blocking and perverting the will of God."* [9]

Understand, if the devil has authority over this earth, which he does, we must wrestle with the next question. What is he doing with this authority? Here's what Jesus says:

"The thief's purpose is to steal, kill, and to destroy" (John 10:10, NLT).

Peter puts it like this:

"Stay alert! Watch out for your great enemy the devil. He prowls around like a roaring lion, looking for someone to devour" (1 Peter 5:8, NLT).

When Adam and Eve sinned in the garden by rebelling against God, sin was unleashed on mankind forever, and the devil was given his authority by God. It is not unlimited authority, and it is not his to do with as he wishes. The devil's authority, even though it is great, is limited. God is still the protective agent over His creation. He is sovereign, and no one can take away God's sovereignty. His general goodness protects us from the enemy totally destroying what He has created. Psalm 104 talks about God's general goodness.

"You make springs pour water into the ravines,
so streams gush down from the mountains.
[11] They provide water for all the animals,
and the wild donkeys quench their thirst.
[12] The birds nest beside the streams
and sing among the branches of the trees.
[13] You send rain on the mountains from your heavenly home,
and you fill the earth with the fruit of your labor.
[14] You cause grass to grow for the livestock
and plants for people to use.
You allow them to produce food from the earth—
[15] wine to make them glad,

olive oil to soothe their skin,
and bread to give them strength" (Psalm 104:10-15, NLT).

Even though you can see the general goodness of God all around you, the devil's authority is still operational, and his authority greatly affects you and me, and it also affects God. God? Yes. We have to understand that we now operate, and God now operates in light of this cursed world. It is not a perfect world, it is a cursed world, with the effects of sin everywhere. I love how C. S. Lewis in his book, *Mere Christianity,* describes this:

"Enemy occupied territory—that is what the world is. Christianity is the story of how the rightful king has landed, you might say landed in disguise, and is calling us to take part in a great campaign of sabotage." [10]

The rightful king now operates in light of this cursed world. Again, it's not a perfect world, it is a cursed world, with the effects of sin everywhere. This is why fasting is so important in the spiritual realm. It, coupled with prayer, unlocks things in the spiritual realm that could not otherwise be unlocked. Let me give you two clear examples of this from the book of Daniel. In Daniel 9, we find Daniel deeply distressed.

"It was the first year of the reign of Darius the Mede, the son of Ahasuerus, who became king of the Babylonians. ² During the first year of his reign, I, Daniel, learned from reading the word of the Lord, as revealed to Jeremiah the prophet, that Jerusalem must lie desolate for seventy years. ³ So I turned to the Lord God and pleaded with him in prayer and fasting. I also wore rough burlap and sprinkled myself with ashes" (Daniel 9:1-3, NLT).

In this encounter, Daniel reads something in the book of Jeremiah about Jerusalem, that it must lie desolate for seventy years. This information was so troubling to Daniel, that he prayed and fasted in order to understand the meaning. Notice what happened the moment Daniel started praying and fasting.

"I went on praying and confessing my sin and the sin of my people,

*pleading with the Lord my God for Jerusalem, his holy mountain. ²¹
As I was praying, Gabriel, whom I had seen in the earlier vision, came
swiftly to me at the time of the evening sacrifice. ²² He explained to
me, "Daniel, I have come here to give you insight and understanding.
²³* **The moment you began praying, a command was given.**
*And now I am here to tell you what it was, for you are very precious to
God. Listen carefully so that you can understand the meaning of your
vision"* (Daniel 9:20-23, NLT, emphasis mine).

Look at that again: *"The moment you began praying, a command was
given."* The moment Daniel began praying and fasting and asking God,
God ordered Gabriel to visit him and to give him the meaning of his
vision. Look now at Daniel chapter 10.

*In the third year of the reign of King Cyrus of Persia, Daniel (also
known as Belteshazzar) had another vision. He understood that the
vision concerned events certain to happen in the future—times of war
and great hardship. ² When this vision came to me, I, Daniel, had been
in mourning for three whole weeks. ³ All that time I had eaten no rich
food. No meat or wine crossed my lips, and I used no fragrant lotions
until those three weeks had passed. ⁴ On April 23, as I was standing on
the bank of the great Tigris River, ⁵ I looked up and saw a man dressed
in linen clothing, with a belt of pure gold around his waist. ⁶ His body
looked like a precious gem. His face flashed like lightning, and his eyes
flamed like torches. His arms and feet shone like polished bronze, and
his voice roared like a vast multitude of people. ⁷ Only I, Daniel, saw
this vision. The men with me saw nothing, but they were suddenly
terrified and ran away to hide. ⁸ So I was left there all alone to see this
amazing vision. My strength left me, my face grew deathly pale, and
I felt very weak. ⁹ Then I heard the man speak, and when I heard the
sound of his voice, I fainted and lay there with my face to the ground.
¹⁰ Just then a hand touched me and lifted me, still trembling, to my
hands and knees. ¹¹ And the man said to me, "Daniel, you are very precious to God, so listen carefully to what I have to say to you. Stand up,
for I have been sent to you." When he said this to me, I stood up, still
trembling. ¹² Then he said, "Don't be afraid, Daniel. Since the first day*

you began to pray for understanding and to humble yourself before your God, your request has been heard in heaven. I have come in answer to your prayer. ¹³ *But for twenty-one days the spirit prince of the kingdom of Persia blocked my way. Then Michael, one of the archangels, came to help me, and I left him there with the spirit prince of the kingdom of Persia.* ¹⁴ *Now I am here to explain what will happen to your people in the future, for this vision concerns a time yet to come"* (Daniel 10:1-14 (NLT).

Okay, what is happening here? Daniel has another vision, but prior to this vision, what had Daniel been doing for three weeks? He had been fasting and praying during that time. Once again, the moment he began praying and fasting, Gabriel appeared to him.

Fasting and praying moves the heavens! This is why God has attached Himself to fasting. It moves Heaven into action, so much so that the *"spirit prince of the kingdom of Persia"* blocked Gabriel from getting to Daniel. Who is this spirit prince? We don't exactly know. We just know it is demonic, and we know that this heavenly battle lasted for 21 days. How many days had Daniel been praying and fasting? 21 days! The angel Michael came at that point to help in this battle, so that Gabriel could come to Daniel.

Now, I'm not making this up. This is a front row seat into spiritual warfare, and what helps to resist the enemy, and to give strength to Heaven's armies, is fasting and praying. Now do you see the importance of praying and fasting? This is why God has attached Himself to it. Fasting unlocks things and releases things in the spiritual world that could not otherwise be unlocked.

You have to understand this as a Christ-follower. This should cause us to begin fasting and praying on a consistent basis, and fasting and praying until God gives us an answer, because we have no idea what is happening in the spiritual world as we pray and fast. Let us wake up and understand that prayer and fasting moves God into action. What is it in your life and in your circumstances that you desperately need to hear from God? Your marriage? Your children? Your job?

Therefore, Pray! Fast! Seek the Lord, and watch Him do things that only He can do. We are living in a spiritual world that is under the control of the evil one. Pray and fast so that God can accomplish His perfect work because God is attached to prayer and fasting.

---

[1] Thomas A. Tarrantson, *"The Place of Fasting in the Christian Life,"* (C. S. Lewis Institute, June 6, 2018), www.cslewisinstitute.org.

[2] Ibid.

[3] Ibid.

[4] Watchman Nee, *"The Prayer Ministry of the Church,"* (Christian Fellowship Publishers, Inc. New York, 1973), 81.

[5] Bill Bright, *"Your Personal Guide to Fasting and Prayer,"* www.cru.org.

[6] Andrew Murry, *"With Christ in the School of Prayer,"* (Fleming H. Revell Company, Toronto, 1895), 98.

[7] Wesley Duewel, *"The Discipline of Fasting,"* www.sermonindex.net.

[8] Ibid.

[9] Phillip Yancey, *"Prayer: Does It Make Any Difference?"* 1st Edition, (Zondervan Books, 2006), 117.

[10] C. S. Lewis, *"Mere Christianity,"* (Harper Collins, 2001), 45-46.

Chapter 5

Attached To Community

In the days of Ancient Rome, Rome would celebrate a major victory with a celebration known as a *"Triumph."* Not every general or leader received one of these triumphs and neither did every battle. There was a very high standard for getting one, but when one was given, it had to have been an awesome sight. First off, the herald would come and announce victory throughout the city saying:

"Roman Victor"

"Rome Has Won"

The people would line the streets in preparation for the general's procession. The returning general would ride in on a grand chariot pulled by many horses. Following him was his victorious army marching along behind him, pulling the carts loaded down with all the spoils of war. Trumpeters would begin playing as the general rode through the streets, and people would begin throwing flowers and petals as he rode by.

As the procession continued, the priests would take the bowls of incense and burn it, and the whole city would be filled with the sweet smell of victory. This is what the Apostle Paul is referring to when he says:

"But thank God! He has made us his captives and continues to lead us along in Christ's triumphal procession. Now he uses us to spread the knowledge of Christ everywhere, like a sweet perfume. 15 Our lives are a Christ-like fragrance rising up to God. But this fragrance is perceived differently by those who are being saved and by those who are perishing. 16 To those who are perishing, we are a dreadful smell of death and doom. But to those who are being saved, we are a life-giving perfume. And who is adequate for such a task as this?" (2 Corinthians 2:14-16, NLT).

Then, to commence forever the victory, they would erect a monument somewhere in the city so that everyone could know and remember what took place. The Arch of Titus in Rome is one of those monuments erected to celebrate Rome's victory over Jerusalem in 70AD. On it are scenes depicting the soldiers carrying away the spoils from the Jewish Temple.

What's interesting about this victory celebration is that the defeated general was usually in the procession as well. They would chain him to the conquering general's chariot. Stripped of his beautiful uniform, they would march him through the city putting him on display in a state of total humiliation.

For those of us who are Christ followers, we are in the victory procession with the Lord. Because of his victory, we are victorious. Because He won, we won. But, there's someone else in that procession. It's the devil, and he's chained to the chariot of Jesus. Yet, instead of us walking in victory and feeling victorious, we often feel like the captive, and we often feel like the devil has the victory. Do you know why we feel this way so often? It is because we are violating a principle, God's principle, for personal victory.

What I am writing about in this chapter will be by far one of the most difficult principles in this book to put into practice because it goes against every human emotion and instinct that we possess. We naturally want to make ourselves look better than we really are. We naturally gravitate toward downplaying our deficits and our flaws, and when it comes to sin, we hide.

There are closet doors in our lives that we want to remain closed to outsiders. Oh, we know about them and we know what lies within them, but that's as far as it goes. There may be the occasional hint to a Pastor or a trusted friend about what's inside, but full admission of what we are really struggling with on the inside is a line that many of us refuse to cross.

All the strongholds, past sins, current struggles and present weaknesses get thrown into that closet. We try to lock it shut promising never to open it again. We say to God and to ourselves, *"This is the last time I'm going to do this"* or *"God, please take this away from me,"* but even as we utter those words to God, the things in the closet continue to grow and call our name. No matter how tightly we try to shut it, the door just keeps coming open. Know what I'm talking about? Ever been there? The Apostle Paul alluded to that closet door when he said,

"So the trouble is not with the law, for it is spiritual and good. The trouble is with me, for I am all too human, a slave to sin. ¹⁵ I don't really understand myself, for I want to do what is right, but I don't do it. Instead, I do what I hate" (Romans 7:14-15, NLT).

Look at the language that Paul uses to describe himself: *"a slave to sin, doing what I hate."* Here's what I want you to understand:

Until you gain victory over that closet door, you will never gain victory in your life.

How then can the battle be won? How do you actually gain victory over that closet door? Is it even possible? Yes, but you have to understand the attachment characteristic of God when it comes to receiving victory in this area.

God is attached to accountability

He's not attached to isolation. That is the very opposite of His character. He's attached to community, specifically in the area of accountability. Remember in the introduction to this book, we agreed that one of the basic understandings of God and how He operates is primarily through the community of people, not the individual. He's attached to community, and victory over sin lies within that context through the means of accountability.

Let me give you something that may be hidden to you at this moment. Sin only grows in the dark, and the power of sin lies in its secrecy. The harder you try to conceal sin, the more it grows, and the more power it receives.

But, what breaks that power? Opening up the closet door and letting in the light! Victory is found in understanding that God is attached to accountability, and I dare write that victory can come no other way based on the following verse that is found in Scripture.

"Therefore confess your sins to each other and pray for each other so that you may be healed. The prayer of a righteous man is powerful and effective" (James 5:16, NIV).

There are two commands, not suggestions, given here for living in community with one another. Confess and pray. The end result of obeying these commands is healing or wholeness. *"So that you may be healed."* In other words, healing means that the closet remains clean and the door remains shut.

Let's dig a little deeper. Did you catch what James is commanding us to confess? Our sin—our shortcomings, our failures, our temptations, our battles, even our sick and twisted desires. In other words, we are commanded to confess to others the junk that we carry around inside of us that we want no one to ever know about. That's what we are commanded to confess to one another.

Some of you are thinking, *"There's no way I would do that. I'd be too embarrassed. Besides, other people don't need to know my dirt. God knows it and that's good enough."*

If that's you then let me gently remind you that this is a command in God's economy. God has attached Himself to accountability, and you cannot violate this Scripture and expect to gain victory. *"Confess your sins to each other...so that you may be healed"* is a command, not a suggestion, and it's the only way to victory. Let's qualify the word *"each other."* Who exactly in the community of faith are we to let in? Look at the Scripture again.

"Therefore confess your sins to each other and pray for each other so that you may be healed. The prayer of a righteous man is powerful and effective" (James 5:16, NIV).

We are not to confess our sins to just anybody. No, we are to confess our sins to righteous people—those who are walking with God. God has set it up this way for several reasons:

Righteous people will indeed pray for you

If they are truly righteous, they will have a high view of prayer because they know that God has attached Himself to it.

Righteous people will have a high view of sin

They will not try to make your sin look better than it is. They will call it what it is.

When I was in seminary, I was the chaplain for the Texas Christian University Horned Frogs baseball team for two seasons. A couple of guys wanted to start a Bible study, so we did. At the very beginning of our first meeting, I suggested that we should each confess something to the group that we were struggling with and then hold each other accountable to that area at the start of every meeting. Everybody thought that seemed like a good idea, so we started each meeting after that by asking each other how we were all doing with our particular vice. It never failed. At every meeting, someone would start defending their sin and justifying their actions when it was their turn to fess up. We all came up with a little chant when that started to happen: *"JUSTIFY, JUSTIFY, JUSTIFY."*

Why do we all push against the practice of accountability and squirm in our seats when we hear it? We do this for a number of reasons:

Pride

The outer façade must look good. We must do whatever it takes to keep up appearances in front of people. All the while, we slowly crumble and rot away on the inside. Look at what Proverbs says about this.

"Pride goes before destruction, a haughty spirit before a fall" (Proverbs 16:18, NIV).

Robert Lewis, in his Men's Fraternity video series says that there are three faces that every person wears—the public face, the private face, and the personal face. The *"public face"* is the face you broadcast to the mass of people around you. It may not be the real you. It may just be the you that you want people to see. The *"private face"* is who you are to a few, close people—like your wife and your children. The *"personal face"* is the REAL you. It's who you really are—the good, the bad, and the ugly.

What Lewis says about these three faces is of critical importance. The closer these faces are and the more the faces look the same, the healthier and the more wholesome a person is. The greater the separation between the *"public face"* that we project, and the real person we are on the inside results in a smaller capacity for real adventure in life, and a greater capacity for real setbacks. Integrity in every one of your faces is the key to a healthy life. [1]

How is that achieved? It is in embracing community inspection, and letting go of pride. Another barrier to this kind of community is:

Fear

The devil has convinced us that we are the only ones that struggle in our area of sin. We cower with fright that someone might gasp at us and reject us if they ever knew what was really going on in the inside of us. The fear of man is so powerful. It keeps us locked up in our prison of secrecy.

My wife and I recently watched a documentary on TV about a fallen Pastor. You might remember him. He founded and pastored a church body of about 14,000 people. At the time this man was president of the National Association of Evangelicals (NAE), an organization that currently represents more than 45,000 local churches, from over forty different denominations and serves a population of millions. [2] At one time, Time Magazine touted him as one of the *"25 most influential evangelicals in America."* [3]

Everything was going great for this Pastor and this church, and then it happened. Seemingly overnight, the walls came crumbling down around him. I remember where I was when I heard the news of his downfall. He had been involved in a grossly immoral relationship dating back to three years earlier. There was drug use involved. It was a messy situation. The day I heard this news, I bowed my head in my office and asked God to keep me from anything like this. *"Dear God, may this never be me. Keep me far from this."*

My wife and I, after we finished watching the documentary, prayed for this man and his family, and then I felt compelled to send him an email to encourage him and to tell him that we had been praying for him. A few days later, I received this reply.

*"Thank you, Pastor. This means the world to me. I appreciate your love, kindness and prayers very much. God bless you in your efforts with the church. You are reflecting the heart of a very good man by taking the time to respond to **A GUY LIKE ME** (emphasis mine) the way you are. I thank God for you."*

How did it all come to this? How did nobody know? Were there no signs pointing to any of this? The saddest thing about this story and this ending is the fact that it is not an isolated incident. Stuff like this happens all the time at churches and in homes all across the world.

I was talking to a friend recently who worked several years for Promise Keepers. He said before the regular men's conference began on Friday night, there was always a conference for Senior Pastors only on Friday morning. The PK staff took an anonymous survey of the Pastors that asked two questions:

1. *Do you have issues with pornography?*

2. *Have you had or are you currently involved in an extra-marital relationship?*

Over 70% of the Pastors answered *"yes"* to one of those two questions. After reading these questionnaires, Promise Keepers changed the programming for the upcoming men's conference literally overnight. There thinking was this, *"If Pastors are struggling in these areas, how many other men are struggling that are not Pastors?*

Let's think about this. Do you think Pastors fear the consequences if they tell someone what's really going on with them? Do you think the devil who is walking in the triumphal procession, defeatedly tied to the chariot of Jesus, is whispering to many of them, *"Keep it to yourself. You can work it out. You can overcome it. You don't need anyone."* By violating the principle of accountability, many people, including Pastors, are held captive with no hope of victory. Another barrier that we face to real community is in the area of:

Deception

We hide many times because we somehow are under the delusion, that what we struggle with is simply not that big of a deal. Isn't it so true? We tend to call sin by a different name which in turn makes ourselves look better than we really are. We're broken people acting like we're not broken. However, we're not the first ones to do this.

Remember Adam and Eve in the Garden of Eden? When God came looking for Adam, he blamed everything on Eve. When He came to Eve, she blamed it on the serpent. It was as if they were saying, *"Certainly I cannot be that bad."* But they were that bad—and so are we. Every one of us is as bad as it gets.

The Bible is an incredible mirror. When held up to our hearts, it reveals things about us that we would normally never see. Look at how the Bible describes the heart of man.

"The LORD observed the extent of human wickedness on the earth, and he saw that everything they thought or imagined was consistently and totally evil" (Genesis 6:5, NLT).

Look at what the prophet Jeremiah says about this.

"The human heart is the most deceitful of all things, and desperately wicked. Who really knows how bad it is? ¹⁰ But I, the LORD, search all hearts and examine secret motives. I give all people their due rewards, according to what their actions deserve" (Jeremiah 17:9-10, NLT).

Notice what Jesus tells the crowd in Matthew 15, with the Pharisees standing right there.

"Anything you eat passes through the stomach and then goes into the sewer. ¹⁸ But the words you speak come from the heart—that's what defiles you. ¹⁹ For from the heart come evil thoughts, murder, adultery, all sexual immorality, theft, lying, and slander" (Matthew 15:17-19, NLT).

Jesus says it's not what you put in your physical body that defiles you, but rather it is what comes out of your heart that defiles you, and evil stuff is found in every human heart. This is why human inspection by others is so valuable. Others can see things in us that we can't see. Without that human inspection and input, the seriousness of sin often remains hidden to us, and deception continues. Again, James 5:16 is a command, not a suggestion from God.

What are the consequences for violating this principle of confession and accountability? Proverbs 5 describes perfectly what happens.

"An evil man is held captive by his own sins; they are ropes that catch and hold him. 23 He will die for lack of self-control; he will be lost because of his great foolishness" (Proverbs 5:22-23, NLT).

Notice the language that Solomon uses. Sin locks us in captivity. It catches us, holds us, and will not let us go. It describes perfectly a stronghold. Solomon even goes on to say that death is the end result!

Although many of us may not directly succumb to death because of our lack of community inspection, our ministry might. Our influence in the community might die, or our relationship with our families or our marriages might end up in death, all because of the violation of a principle that God has put in place.

"Back in 1958 a small community in northeastern Pennsylvania built a little red brick building that was to be their police department, their fire department, and their city hall. They were proud of that building; it was the result of sacrificial giving and careful planning. When the building was completed, they had a ribbon cutting ceremony, and more than six thousand people were there—nearly all the town's residents. It was the biggest event of the year.

Within less than two months, however, they began to notice some ominous cracks on the side of this red brick building. Sometime later, it was noticed that the windows would not shut all the way. Then it was discovered that the doors wouldn't close correctly. Eventually the floor shifted and left ugly gaps in the floor covering and corners. The roof began to leak. Within a few more months, it had to be evacuated, to the embarrassment of the builder and the disgust of the taxpayers.

A firm did an analysis shortly thereafter and found that the blasts from a nearby mining area were slowly but effectively destroying the building. Imperceptibly, down beneath the foundation, there were small shifts and changes taking place that caused the whole foundation to crack. You couldn't feel it or even see it from the surface, but quietly and down deep there was a weakening. A city official finally had to write across the door of that building, 'Condemned. Not fit for public use.' Ultimately the building had to be demolished." 4

There is a moral for all of us within that story. Outward troubles appear when our inner moral foundation begins to shift and crack. If there is no one there to help regularly inspect the foundation, the results can often be catastrophic—*"Condemned. Not fit for public use,"* which is the devil's goal for every one of God's children.

In my previous church, I became very good friends with a guy. We did so much together and spent a lot of time together, talking about the Lord and what He was doing in our lives. But soon, things began to change in our relationship. He started pulling back and withdrawing from me. Our conversations got shorter and shorter and our regular late-night talks after our elder meetings began to stop. Oh, there was always a legitimate excuse, and I always took him at his word. Why wouldn't I? This went on for a few months, and I suspected nothing wrong, until I got a phone call.

His wife shared with me that she had just found out that he had been having an affair for the last several months. She had proof, and his confession later to me confirmed my biggest nightmare. I was devastated. How could this happen? We were so close. We ministered for years side by side. We talked on a daily basis. We sat through elder meetings together and prayed together. Why didn't I know? The environment in our elder meetings was there for him to share his struggles and temptations with us. The environment in our friendship was there for him to be open and honest with me, but instead of acting on the principle of confession, he sat in silence and slowly let his sin overtake him.

Don't let this be your story. God has attached Himself to accountability. You cannot violate God's principle and expect to walk in victory. It is only when light is shed on the closet, the confession of sin to another, that sin withers and dies. It is the accountability of people that leads to victory in your life. Sin only grows in the dark. Therefore, whatever you are dealing with, get it out and in the open. Shine the light on it, and let God heal you through accountability.

[1] Robert Lewis *"Men's Fraternity: The Great Adventure: Session 9: Being Advised of Adventure Busters Part 1,"* (Lifeway, Nashville, 2005), 33.

[2] National Association of Evangelicals. www.nae.org.

[3] Time Staff, *"The 25 Most Influential Evangelicals in America,"* (February 07, 2005), www.content.time.com.

[4] Charles R. Swindoll, *"Hand Me Another Brick,"* (Bantam Books, New York, 1988), 80.

Chapter 6

Attached to Obedience

Let me give you a real picture of what a true follower of Christ undergoes throughout his or her journey with the Lord. When a person comes to Christ, his life looks like a dining room table with a big mess on it—clutter, crumbs, things that need to be thrown away. This is what the Holy Spirit immediately begins working on.

He doesn't say, *"Clean up before you come to Me."* He says, *"Come to Me and let me clean you,"* and once the table is cleared by Him of the visible clutter, He then starts working on the crevasses. He searches out every little piece of dirt in order to make us look exactly like the Lord Jesus Christ. This is what the Christian life is. It is a never-ending process of inspection by our Lord and Master, and here's the deal. What God says to do, you do. What He says to get rid of, you get rid of it. Obeying God is not optional for a true child of God, because God is attached to obedience.

When God says to do something, you don't say: *"Well, let me pray about that." "Let me see if this is right." "Let me see if it works with my schedule."* You say, "Yes" and you watch the Lord do a wonderful work. Why is it sometimes difficult to obey the Lord? Can I tell you why? It comes down to one word:

Trust

We don't trust that God knows best. We don't trust that He knows what He is doing. It comes down to the fact that we don't really trust Him. And why is it that we don't trust Him fully and completely?

Know

It is because we don't fully know Him. Knowing Him leads to trusting Him. Think about this: Would you automatically trust someone that you don't really know? Probably not. The same is true with God. You cannot really trust God until you really know God, but what happens when you know God and trust God? To where does that lead?

Obedience

It leads to one place, obedience. Here's what you begin to understand as you obey the Lord over and over. You understand that God is right. You understand that God's way is best. You understand that what God says to do works, and the more you begin to obey Him, the more you begin to know Him and trust Him, and the more you begin to understand that the blessings of God are opened to you when you do what He says because He is attached to obedience.

It doesn't take anyone going through the Scriptures very much time to see that God has attached Himself to obedience. It is very obvious. When you obey, you thrive. When you disobey, you suffer the consequences of going your own way. Again, the things that God has said in his Word are not up for debate.

Obedience is never cafeteria style, *"I'll take a little of that and this, but hold those."* That seemed to be the case for Thomas Jefferson who read his King James Bible with a razor blade in hand. He cut out the virgin birth, all the miracles—including the most important one, the Resurrection—then pasted together what was left and called it *The Life and*

Morals of Jesus of Nazareth. [1]

You can't do that with obedience. God expects us to fully obey Him in every area of our lives. Let me show you this understanding at work in the Scriptures. Right before the children of Israel are about to enter into the Promised Land, Moses tells them about the blessing of obedience and the curse of disobedience.

"If you fully obey the Lord your God and carefully keep all his commands that I am giving you today, the Lord your God will set you high above all the nations of the world. [2] *You will experience all these blessings if you obey the Lord your God:*

[3] *Your towns and your fields*
　　will be blessed.
[4] *Your children and your crops*
　　will be blessed.
The offspring of your herds and flocks
　　will be blessed.
[5] *Your fruit baskets and breadboards*
　　will be blessed.
[6] *Wherever you go and whatever you do,*
　　you will be blessed" (Deuteronomy 28:1-6, NLT).

Did you see it once again? It's the *"If/Then"* statement of God. He tells them plainly, in detail, what all the blessings are that He plans on giving them IF they follow the instructions of the Lord and obey Him. But, look at the next verses of that same chapter.

"But if you refuse to listen to the Lord your God and do not obey all the commands and decrees I am giving you today, all these curses will come and overwhelm you:

[16] *Your towns and your fields*
　　will be cursed.
[17] *Your fruit baskets and breadboards*
　　will be cursed.

18 Your children and your crops
will be cursed.
The offspring of your herds and flocks
will be cursed.
19 Wherever you go and whatever you do,
you will be cursed" (Deuteronomy 28:15-19, NLT).

He said that the refusal of obedience to God will result in curses! God is attached to obedience, and obedience is always attached to blessing. *"If you obey Me, I will bless you."* Disobedience is always attached to a curse. *"If you don't obey Me, I will curse you."* I believe this is how God works. He blesses obedience, and He can never bless disobedience. Never. Deuteronomy 30 states the choice that He gives the people of Israel.

"Now listen! Today I am giving you a choice between life and death, between prosperity and disaster. 16 For I command you this day to love the Lord your God and to keep his commands, decrees, and regulations by walking in his ways. If you do this, you will live and multiply, and the Lord your God will bless you and the land you are about to enter and occupy" (Deuteronomy 30: 15-16, NLT, emphasis mine).

Isn't this the same choice that we've been facing since the beginning of time? Adam and Eve faced this same choice, and we face this same choice every day. Obey God and live and prosper and be blessed, disobey and suffer the consequences.

I've begun to look at sin in a broader range. Light and dark not right or wrong. Let me explain. We love to push the boundaries when it comes to sin. *"Is there a rule against it?"* *"Does the Bible specifically forbid it?"* If nothing can be found, then we march ahead into it. That's the *"right or wrong"* mentality. It's an okay system to live by, but it's not the best.

The best system is the *"light and dark"* system. Here's how it works: If you have to conceal what you are doing, keep it covered up, keep it hush-hush, dim the lights for, lower your voice for, sneak around for, go around the corner for, (the list could go on and on) should you really be doing it? It may not be *"sin"* in the black and white sense, but is it something that Jesus would do? Is it initiated and okayed by God? I mean, should you really say something about someone unless it can be shouted out loud? How many times have you had to lower your voice or cover your mouth just to say something negative about another person? It may be a truthful statement, but why is it necessary to conceal it? See what I mean? Maybe, because it has to be done *"in the dark,"* it is sin and disobedience after all.

"If we claim to have fellowship with him yet walk in the darkness, we lie and do not live by the truth. ⁷ But if we walk in the light, as he is in the light, we have fellowship with one another, and the blood of Jesus, his Son, purifies us from all sin" (1 John 1:6-7, NIV).

The book of 1 John says to *"Walk in the light as he is in the light."* If it can't be done in the light, then maybe it shouldn't be done at all. This is, by far, the most dangerous aspect of sin. It's deceptive and crafty just like its author. Sometimes sin has just a hint of light to it that makes us see it as right in our own eyes. This is why we must walk in the light when it comes to full obedience.

There's a story about a father who was looking to hire a stagecoach driver to transport his family safely into town. They lived on a high overlook that had many dangerous turns on the way up and down. For every stagecoach driver that he interviewed, he asked each one the same question.

"Sir, how close can you get to the edge can you get before taking my family over the cliff?"

The first one answered, *"Sir, I can get two feet from the edge. I'm a very good driver."*

The next one answered, *"Sir, I can get one foot from the edge without going over. I'm an excellent driver."*

The third man heard the question and responded differently than all the others. Because of his response, he was hired on the spot. What did he say? How did he answer the father's question?

He simply said this, *"My good man, the question is not how close to the edge can I get without going over? The question is how far away from the edge can I possibly get?"*

The same is true for us and sin. Our attitude should always be in keeping with the driver who actually got the job. *"It's not a matter of how close to the edge I can get before I go over. It's all about getting as far from the edge as I possibly can."*

Obedience is hearing the Word of God and putting it into practice. It is doing what He says from a heart of love. This is not obedience out of duty or obligation. The Christian knows of no such thing. Obedience to God is not burdensome or heavy. It is with joy that we obey the Lord.

How could we, with the view of the cross that we have, see obedience to God as anything but a blessing? How could we, who have now received the Holy Spirit, do anything else? Before we came to Christ, we longed to disobey. But, after coming to Christ, we, now with joy, long to obey Him, because God is attached to obedience and has placed that obedience in our hearts through the Holy Spirit. It is our highest privilege. Look at what Jesus says in Mark 11.

"But even more blessed are all who hear the word of God and put it into practice" (Mark 11:28, NIV).

All who hear the Word of God and obey it, are considered what? Blessed. Jesus goes a little further saying, *"More blessed."* This is the reward for obeying God, since it is our highest privilege.

This is not prosperity preaching. Prosperity preachers qualify the blessings by saying that God is obliged to bless you financially, or physically when you obey Him; a health and wealth doctrine.

Let me ask you, *"Does the Bible promise this to every person? Health and wealth?"* No, but the Bible does promise blessings for obedience, and just because this has been twisted and misused by so many preachers who simply want to line their own pockets with money, it does not nullify the Scriptural understanding:

God is attached to obedience.

Obedience is attached to blessing.

You say to yourself, *"Okay, Pastor Matt. I hear you, but what kind of blessings does God give when we obey?"* I want you to think about a parent child relationship for one moment. Suppose your child came to you and said:

"Mom and Dad. The only thing I want in this life, from this moment on, is to obey your every word. Whatever you tell me to do, I will do, and whatever you tell me to stay away from, I will. My desire is to only do your will."

Now, after you've picked yourself up off of the ground, would you then say to them, *"Get out of my sight!"* Would you say that? Would you say to them, *"You are such a disappointment to me?"* Would you curse them in any way? Why would you not? Because they have set their mind to completely obey you.

If your child actually came to you and said this to you with all sincerity, what would you do?

Would you expand their privileges?

Would you give them more trust?

Would you give them more blessings?

Would you try to bless them as much as possible?

You would go out of your way to bless them, and the blessings are too numerous to list, isn't that right?

Would you give them more freedom?

Would you honor them?

Would you want to make them as happy as possible?

Why? So that they can dutifully obey you? No! The desire in their heart is already there. Why then would you go out of your way to bless them? As a reward! It is the reward of blessing coming from you as joy fills your heart because they finally get it! Isn't that right?

Understand that God is the same way, and yet He is so much greater! He loves it when we obey. Do you know what it communicates to God when we obey Him? Exactly what we've been saying all along: That we trust Him. That we believe Him. That we acknowledge that His way is best. Why wouldn't He be delighted to shower us with blessings?

This was true in Peter's life. Remember when Jesus climbed into Peter's boat and began to teach the crowds from there? The story is found in Luke chapter 5.

"One day as Jesus was preaching on the shore of the Sea of Galilee, great crowds pressed in on him to listen to the word of God. ² He noticed two empty boats at the water's edge, for the fishermen had left them and were washing their nets. ³ Stepping into one of the boats, Jesus asked Simon, its owner, to push it out into the water. So he sat in the boat and taught the crowds from there" (Luke 5:1-3, NLT).

This was a seemingly insignificant task that Jesus asked of Peter. *"Push Me out into the water,"* and Peter obeyed. What was the blessing attached to his obedient response? There were two.

He was in the center of God's will

Think about that. In that moment of simple obedience, He was with Jesus, and being with Jesus and doing what Jesus is doing is directly in the center of God's will, don't you think? Secondly,

He was used by God

By obeying Jesus in this little request, he was used in Jesus' ministry. His *"Yes"* paved the way for others to hear the message of Jesus. Look at what happens next in the story.

When he had finished speaking, he said to Simon, "Now go out where it is deeper, and let down your nets to catch some fish." 5 "Master," Simon replied, "we worked hard all last night and didn't catch a thing. But if you say so, I'll let the nets down again" (Luke 5:4-5, NLT).

In this culture, fishing was done at night. The fish would come into shallow water at night, and the fishermen would throw their nets to catch them. In the daytime the fish would go back out into deeper water, and they were much harder to catch. Everybody knew that! Seemingly everyone but Jesus!

Peter had just finished cleaning his nets, and now they were going to get dirty all over again for nothing. He was going to have to clean them again even though he was probably dead tired from being out all night. Do you think there was a pause when he told Jesus about the night fishing rule? I can picture them just staring at each other in that boat. Peter thinking to himself, *"I'm the master fisherman,"* and Jesus thinking about Peter, *"You know I AM the Master, right?"*

I love what Peter says to Jesus. *"But if You say so..."* That is so good. *"I'll do it, Lord, not because I agree with it or think it's a good idea but just because You say so,"* and God certainly had a lot to say when this interaction was all over. Look at the next few verses.

"And this time their nets were so full of fish they began to tear! 7 A shout for help brought their partners in the other boat, and soon both boats were filled with fish and on the verge of sinking" (Luke 5:6-7, NLT).

What were the blessings this time on the other side of obedience? Again, there were two.

Material blessing

When they threw their nets in the water, there were so many fish that the nets began to tear! There were so many fish that they almost sunk two boats! Would you say that this was a supernatural, physical blessing? Sometimes God does bless you in a material way, and that is not outside the realm of something that God wants to do. Afterall, we live in a physical, material world, and God does want to bless us with good things. But, but, but, that is not the real blessing in the story. What was the reason in Peter's life for the extravagant material blessing?

When Simon Peter realized what had happened, he fell to his knees before Jesus and said, "Oh, Lord, please leave me—I'm too much of a sinner to be around you." [9] *For he was awestruck by the number of fish they had caught, as were the others with him* (Luke 5:8-9 (NLT).

Here is the real reason for the miraculous number of fish. It was the second blessing that he received.

Spiritual blessing

After Peter obeyed and after God overwhelmingly blessed him with the catch of fish, Peter experienced God in a way that he had never done so before. His eyes were opened, and they weren't looking at all of the fish that were caught. They were open and looking face to face at God being in his boat, and it scared him to death.

The physical blessing no longer mattered! The greatest blessing for Peter was not the catch of fish. It was that he couldn't take his eyes off of the Lord! As a matter of fact, He left the fish to follow the Lord! Did you know that?

The end of the story says that Peter, James and John left everything to follow Jesus. Nothing is mentioned about the fish, the physical blessing! They didn't stop and clean them or pack them in ice, or take them home to put away. They left them to follow after Jesus! This was Peter's real treasure! He had seen the Lord, and that was all that mattered to him.

This is the reason for any physical blessing that comes into our lives. It is so we can fall to our knees in worship and awe of our great God. God has attached Himself to obedience, may it always lead us back to Him, the greatest blessing!

---

[1] R.P. Nettelhorst, *"Notes on the Founding Fathers and the Separation of Church and State,"* (Quartz Hill School of Theology, October 2017), www.theology.edu.

Chapter 7

Attached To The Orphan and Widow

James 1:27 is the verse that every follower of Jesus needs to commit to memory if they have not already done so. Before we get to the verse, I want to shed some light on who wrote the verse. The book of James is written by James, the brother of Jesus. This means that James and Jesus ate at the same table. This means that James got to see all that Jesus did. After Jesus rises from the dead, and after Jesus appears to him, James finally believes and worships Jesus as LORD. Notice the initial greeting in his letter

"This letter is from James, a slave of God and of the Lord Jesus Christ" (James 1:1, NLT).

What a transformation! He's changed from being a skeptic of his brother to now considering himself to be a slave to his brother, the Lord Jesus Christ! Now, he's writing this letter as a leader of the Church to believers scattered throughout the Roman Empire. One of the major themes in the book of James is this: *"Faith, without works, is dead."*

He does not mean in this statement that in order to have faith, you have to work for it and earn it. No! He's saying that genuine faith will express itself outwardly. It is proof that Christ has come to live in a person's life. He summarizes this argument in the last verse of chapter two.

"Just as the body is dead without breath, so also faith is dead without good works" (James 2:26, NLT).

When the Holy Spirit comes into a person, when the breath of God per se comes in and makes a person alive, He will show Himself outwardly toward others in the form of good works. What kind of good works does James, the brother of Jesus, have in mind? Look at James 1:27.

"Pure and genuine religion in the sight of God the Father means caring for orphans and widows in their distress and refusing to let the world corrupt you" (James 1:27 (NLT).

James, who lived with Jesus and grew up with Jesus, says that the outward manifestation of the Holy Spirit inside of a person's life in the form of good works will be directed toward the work of caring for the orphan and the widow.

Why does the Holy Spirit move us toward the orphan and the widow? Because God has attached Himself to these very people. When we care for them, we are actually caring for the Lord! Don't miss that. God is attached to the orphan and the widow. Let's briefly examine this verse:

Orphans and widows: the fatherless and husbandless

At the time that James was writing this in the early part of the first century, if these two groups of people were left to themselves, they were reduced to: begging, stealing, selling themselves and starving.

They are representative of the most marginalized, disenfranchised, on the fringe, vulnerable, taken advantage of, helpless people on the face of the earth. James says to the early Christians and to us: put your eyes and focus right here on them.

Caring for in their distress

"Caring for" is not a social call or a wave or a pop-in visit. It is the understanding that we assume responsibility for them and their distress-

ful situation, and give them the means of support. Interestingly, it's the same word used to describe Jesus found in Luke's Gospel.

"Praise the Lord, the God of Israel, because he has visited (cared for) and redeemed his people" (Luke 1:68, NLT).

Jesus didn't just pop in or wave to us. He lived among us and died for us. In the same way, it is caring for them and assuming responsibility for them, as Jesus cared for and visited humanity.

Refusing to let the world corrupt you

So often we focus solely on the first part of this verse (caring for orphans and widows), but there is a giant *"and"* in that verse.

Caring for the orphan and the widow

AND

Refusing to let the world corrupt you.

What does James mean by *"world"* here? It is the total system of evil that is in opposition of God and His righteous ways. It is what the world exalts: money, power and pleasure. James, the brother of Jesus, is screaming at us: *"Don't adopt the world's value system. Don't be corrupted by the world. Keep your eyes focused on the orphan and the widow, because God is attached to them. When you find them, you find Him. When you help them, you help Him."*

Pure and genuine religion in the site of God

The word *"religion"* is misleading. I believe the best way to translate this word is by using the word *"worship."* With that as our understanding, here's what James is saying:

The purest, most genuine way to worship God is to detach from the world so that you can attach to the orphan and widow.

Think about this. God is saying:

"This is how I want you to worship Me above all else."

"This is what I supremely desire."

"This is what My heart beats most for."

"This is what supremely pleases Me the most, to care for the orphan and the widow."

A few weeks ago, while I was on a board retreat for a non-profit that focuses on fulfilling James 1:27, caring for widows and orphans in their distress, I shared with them Isaiah 1. Why Isaiah 1? Look at what God says to the people of Judah.

"Listen to the Lord, you leaders of "Sodom." Listen to the law of our God, people of "Gomorrah." [11] *"What makes you think I want all your sacrifices?" says the Lord. "I am sick of your burnt offerings of rams and the fat of fattened cattle. I get no pleasure from the blood of bulls and lambs and goats.* [12] *When you come to worship me, who asked you to parade through my courts with all your ceremony?* [13] *Stop bringing me your meaningless gifts; the incense of your offerings disgusts me! As for your celebrations of the new moon and the Sabbath and your special days for fasting—they are all sinful and false. I want no more of your pious meetings.* [14] *I hate your new moon celebrations and your annual festivals. They are a burden to me. I cannot stand them!* [15] *When you lift up your hands in prayer, I will not look. Though you offer many prayers, I will not listen, for your hands are covered with the blood of innocent victims.* [16] ***Wash yourselves and be clean! Get your sins out of my sight. Give up your evil ways.*** [17] ***Learn to do good. Seek justice. Help the oppressed. Defend the cause of orphans. Fight for the rights of widows"*** (Isaiah 1:10-17, NLT, emphasis mine).

The people said, *"God, we will worship you in this way,"* and God says, *"I don't want to be worshipped in an empty ritual and pompous ceremony. This is what I want! I want you to keep yourselves clean from sin, and defend the cause of the orphan and the widow."*

Have you ever told somebody what to get you for a present? They asked you, maybe for your birthday or Christmas, and you told them exactly what you wanted? You sent them the link. You circled it in the catalog. One of my children, around the time of her birthday, makes a list of what she wants and puts in on the refrigerator! She lets everyone know what she wants.

What if, instead of getting her what is on her list, what if we just randomly bought her something instead? Do you think she would be happy? Do you think she would say, *"Wow. Thanks,"* or do you think she might be confused and disappointed? This is what God is asking for, begging for, *"Worship Me in this way. I've attached Myself to them. Go and rescue them."*

The Gospel has always been about rescuing the sinner, rescuing the vulnerable, caring for the sick, the down and out, the helpless. It's exactly what Jesus has done for us. Because of the ravaging effects of sin, we were needy, we were helpless, we were sick, we were wounded, we were lost and hopeless and Jesus found us, rescued us, and saved us. And He, living inside of us, is compelling us to go to them.

Here's the impact of what James is saying and what Isaiah is saying: *"The purest, most genuine way to worship God is to detach from the world so that you can attach to the orphan and widow."* It cannot be any clearer. God says, *"I want you to worship Me in this way, because I am attached to the orphan and the widow. When you find them, you will find Me because I'm attached to them."*

To these is to whom God is attached, all 153 million of them in the world right now. Seriously, don't gloss over these verses in Isaiah 1 and James 1:27. Spend time in them. Ask the Holy Spirit to show you how He wants to apply it to your life. God is attached to the orphan and the widow. Attach yourselves to them and find Him there.

Chapter 8

Attached To Giving

Mark Twain was once attributed as saying, *"Some people are troubled by the things in the Bible they can't understand. The things that trouble me are the things I can understand."* [1] To follow that up, what troubles me is what Jesus says about being rich.

Then Jesus said to his disciples, "I tell you the truth, it is very hard for a rich person to enter the Kingdom of Heaven. [24] *I'll say it again—it is easier for a camel to go through the eye of a needle than for a rich person to enter the Kingdom of God!"* (Matthew 19:23-24, NLT).

Trust me. When His disciples heard this, they looked at each other in utter confusion.

The disciples were astounded. "Then who in the world can be saved?" they asked (Matthew 19:25, NLT).

When we think of rich, we constantly look up to the person ahead of us like Elon Musk, who as of 2023 is considered to be the richest person in the world, worth upwards of $224 billion. [2] Now that guy is rich! Yet, how does the Bible define rich?

More than adequate shelter,

More than two changes of clothes,

More food in your house than what you will eat today.

With that as the definition, how rich then are you, and how rich am I? I went to globalrichlist.com to see where I rank in world wealth. Do you know where I rank in world wealth? I am in the top 1% of the of world! I am financially ahead of over 99% of all the people on the planet! There are only about 55 million people ahead of me in wealth! With over 8 billion people on the planet, I rank ahead of over 7 billion, 945 million people! I know what you are saying to yourself, *"Wow, you must be rich."* No. What you need to understand is just how poor the rest of the world really is.

Americans own approximately 31% of the world's wealth, [3] but comprise only 4% of the world's population. [4] The average American consumes as much as 370 Ethiopians do. [5] Incomes have gone up over 17% in the last 40 years, [6] while giving to charity has gone down to the lowest it has been since 1995. [7] Let that sink in.

Getting up,

Giving down

According to trusted research,

5% of people tithe, [8] and 9% of those who are *"born again"* tithe. [9]

I've spoken with several overseas mission organizations who work with some of the poorest communities in the world, and they all tell me the same thing. Churches in the U.S. are pulling back their overseas resources in order to *"help"* people in their American communities. I wonder if they have any idea how poor people are around the world and just how rich every American truly is?

"Pastor Matt, why are you making such a big deal about this? You know that people get funny when you talk about money. Does this really matter to God?"

The reason that I'm making a big deal about this is because, God is attached to giving, and things are unlocked when we step over into the realm of generosity. Look at what it says in the book of Proverbs.

"Give freely and become more wealthy;
  be stingy and lose everything.

²⁵ *The generous will prosper;*
  those who refresh others will themselves be refreshed" (Proverbs 11:24-25, NLT).

Divine economics doesn't work through getting. Divine economics works through giving. *"The generous will prosper."* Look at what Jesus said in Luke's Gospel.

"And don't be concerned about what to eat and what to drink. Don't worry about such things. ³⁰ These things dominate the thoughts of unbelievers all over the world, but your Father already knows your needs. ³¹ Seek the Kingdom of God above all else, and he will give you everything you need" (Luke 12:29-31, NLT).

Seek the Kingdom above all else, and God will give you everything you need. I love what Paul tells the Corinthian church in regards to the love offering they were about to send to the believers in Jerusalem.

"Remember this—a farmer who plants only a few seeds will get a small crop. But the one who plants generously will get a generous crop. ⁷ You must each decide in your heart how much to give. And don't give reluctantly or in response to pressure. "For God loves a person who gives cheerfully." ⁸ And God will generously provide all you need. Then you will always have everything you need and plenty left over to share with others" (2 Corinthians 9:6-8, NLT).

There it is again. The reason why God will generously provide all you need is because God is attached to giving. He gives to you, when you give to Him.

A few days ago, I was reading in Acts 10 about the interaction between Cornelius, a Gentile military commander, and Peter, a devout Jewish believer. In this interaction, God tells Peter to go to Cornelius' house. Why? Why command him to go to the house of a Gentile? Look at the passage.

*In Caesarea there lived a Roman army officer named Cornelius, who was a captain of the Italian Regiment. ² He was a devout, God-fearing man, as was everyone in his household. He gave generously to the poor and prayed regularly to God. ³ One afternoon about three o'clock, he had a vision in which he saw an angel of God coming toward him. "Cornelius!" the angel said. ⁴ Cornelius stared at him in terror. "What is it, sir?" he asked the angel. And the angel replied, **"Your prayers and gifts to the poor have been received by God as an offering!** ⁵ Now send some men to Joppa, and summon a man named Simon Peter. ⁶ He is staying with Simon, a tanner who lives near the seashore"* (Acts 10:1-6, NLT, emphasis mine).

God saw this Gentile's gifts to the poor, who had yet to come to Christ, as an offering to Him, and I believe that God sent an angelic messenger in response to Cornelius' generosity. Why would God do that? It is because God has attached Himself to giving, and He is moved by it.

The best example of God being attached to giving is found in Malachi 3. Notice what the Lord tells the priests and the people:

"Should people cheat God? Yet you have cheated me! "But you ask, 'What do you mean? When did we ever cheat you?' "You have cheated me of the tithes and offerings due to me" (Malachi 3:8, NLT).

God tells the people and the priests that they have been cheating Him or robbing Him. How have they done this? By withholding the tithes and offerings due to Him. Notice that phrase, *"Due to Him."* What does that mean? When something is due, it's no longer voluntary. It's owed. When it comes to God, the tithes and the offerings are owed to God. Why is that? Because God is a God of first portions. If you look through the Bible, you will notice that God told the people that:

The first day of the week belonged to Him,

The first born belonged to Him,

The first portion of the field belonged to Him,

The first portion of the livestock belonged to Him,

The first city belonged to Him.

The first of everything that the Israelites owned, belonged to Him, and when something belongs to someone else, you return it. At that point, it's no longer a gift given. It is something that is due back to the Lord. This is how God views giving, and when we don't give Him back what belongs to Him, He considers it robbery, and He will not bless it.

"You are under a curse, for your whole nation has been cheating me" (Malachi 3:9, NLT).

God said that the nation has been put under a curse because they have been careless with the tithes and offerings due to the Lord. When you rob God of the tithe and offering due to Him, you rob Him of the chance to work in your life. You invite Him to leave your situation. It's not that God doesn't want to bless you, it's that He can't. Go back and read that again. He can't bless you because you are violating a principle in the Word of God. God is attached to giving. Notice His solution:

"Bring all the tithes into the storehouse so there will be enough food in my Temple. If you do," says the Lord of Heaven's Armies, "I will open the windows of heaven for you. I will pour out a blessing so great you won't have enough room to take it in!" (Malachi 3:10, NLT).

Why will God open up the windows of heaven? Why will God pour out such a blessing that there won't be enough room to take it in? It is because we rightfully give back what belongs to Him.

Can I tell you why this is so important? When we trust God with the tithe, when we see that it truly belongs to Him, there is an element of faith in that transaction. Isn't that right? It causes us to stop trusting in ourselves, and instead it becomes the beginning point of trust in God. It gets our eyes off of possessing things, because if we are not careful, our possessions can begin to possess us. David Platt in his book, Radical, says this:

"The war against materialism in our hearts is exactly that: a war. It is a constant battle to resist the temptation to have more luxuries, to ac-

quire more stuff, and to live more comfortably. It requires strong and steady resolve to live the gospel in the middle of an American dream that identifies success as moving up the ladder, getting the bigger and better house, purchasing the nicer car, buying the better clothes, eating the finer food, and acquiring more things." [10]

John the Apostle says it like this:

"Do not love the world or anything in the world. If anyone loves the world, the love of the Father is not in him. [16] For everything in the world—the cravings of sinful man (The lust of the flesh), the lust of his eyes and the boasting of what he has and does (The pride of life)— comes not from the Father but from the world" (1 John 2:15-16, NIV).

The last verse in the book of 1 John says this:

"Dear children, keep yourselves from idols" (1 John 5:21, NIV).

In other words, keep yourselves away from anything that might take God's place in your hearts. This is the battle we all face. Especially when it comes to materialism. As Martin Luther said,

"There are three conversions necessary: the conversion of the heart, the conversion of the mind, and the conversion of the purse." [11]

An "unconverted purse" is you looking at your present finances and saying, "I can't afford to let that portion go." When your purse is converted, you begin to think, "There is no way I can afford NOT to let that portion go and be returned to God."

When you trust God and return what is due to Him, God shows up in your life. He is faithful to the "If/Then" statement. If you do, I will, and He does! One of the greatest illustrations that I've seen about giving back to God is demonstrated with a cantaloupe. What's inside of a cantaloupe? Seeds. When you bring that first portion back to God, God opens it and He begins depositing those seeds into every area of your life: financially, spiritually, and relationally. This is divine economics and God is faithful to it. This is why he says the next statement:

"Try it! Put me to the test!" (Malachi 3:10b, NLT).

This is the only time in Scripture that God dares His people to obey Him. He says, *"I dare you to trust Me in this."* Think about that. Why would He say that concerning the area of giving? It is because God has attached Himself to giving. Notice the results:

"Your crops will be abundant, for I will guard them from insects and disease. Your grapes will not fall from the vine before they are ripe," says the Lord of Heaven's Armies (Malachi 3:11, NLT).

God says, *"I will guard them. Invite Me into your situation through giving and I will work for you not against you."* Back to the cantaloupe. What happens if you let a cantaloupe just sit there? If it remains unopened and unused, what eventually happens? It rots and it spoils. That's what God is alluding to here. *"Bring back to Me what is rightfully mine. When you do, I will do even more than you can even think or even imagine."*

What's the greatest blessing when we give? Do you know what it is? It is the Lord, just like Peter realized a few chapters earlier! It is the Lord God with us! It is Him saying about our obedience in this area: *"I will guard them."* The greatest blessing from giving is getting God Himself.

Understand clearly. You will never have God's full blessing until you become a giver. You will never have God's best until you become a giver. You will constantly live under His curse for refusing to give back to Him what is due Him, because He has no other choice. He's attached to giving! Therefore, don't hold back the tithe. Give it to Him and more, and watch Him work in your life and in your circumstances.

---

[1] Mark Twain, *Watertown Daily Times* (Watertown, New York, February 6, 1915), Page 12, Column 6.

[2] Bloomberg Billionaires Index, (2023), www.bloomberg.com/billionaires.

[3] Sport of Money, *"How Rich Are Americans On A Global Scale? Very Rich!,"* (October 31, 2022), www.sportofmoney.com.

[4] Worldometer, *United States Population,* (July 16, 2023), www.worldometer.info.

[5] Washington State University, *"Consumption by the United States,"* (2008), www.public.wsu.edu.

[6] Juhohn Lee, *"Why American wages haven't grown despite increases in productivity,"* (July 19, 2022), www.cnbc.com.

[7] Ivana Saric, *"Americans are giving to charity at lowest level in nearly 3 decades,"* (Jun 22, 2023), www.axios.com.

[8] Denis Greene, *"On Tithing: How Many Church Members Tithe?"* (April 3, 2019), www.church-development.com.

[9] George Barna, *"New Study Shows Trends in Tithing and Donating,"* (April 14, 2008), www.barna.com.

[10] David Platt, *"Radical: Taking Back Your Faith from the American Dream,"* (Multnomah, 1st Edition, 2010), 136.

[11] Jonathan K. Dodson, *"You Are Being Changed for the Good of the Church,"* (October 29, 2019), www.crossway.org.

Chapter 9

Attached To Thanksgiving

Someone has correctly asked, *"What if you only got to keep tomorrow what you thanked God for today?"* That's a good word that needs to be written down and seen often. In your mind, stop and ponder this question: *"What am I thankful for right now?"*

Are you thankful for your relationship with God?

Are you thankful for your family and friends?

Are you thankful for your health if you are blessed with that?

Are you thankful for the clothes that you are wearing, or the place where you live?

Are you thankful for the good things that you enjoy, along with the thousands of things that we take for granted every single day?

The book of Proverbs says that ears to hear and eyes to see are gifts from the Lord. Are you thankful for the ability to hear and see?

Again, what if you only got to keep tomorrow what you thanked God for today? How important would thanksgiving to God become to you on a daily basis if you knew this was true? Do you know that giving thanks to God is so important to Him that He commanded for it to be given?

"Give thanks in all circumstances; for this is the will of God in Christ Jesus for you" (1 Thessalonians 5:18, ESV).

What is the will of God for every person? It is to give thanks in all circumstances. This is what we are commanded to do.

"Give thanks to the Lord, for he is good! His faithful love endures forever" (Psalm 107:1, NLT).

"Enter his gates with thanksgiving; go into his courts with praise. Give thanks to him and praise his name" (Psalm 100:4, NLT).

We are commanded to give thanks to Him and enter His presence with thanksgiving on our lips.

"Don't worry about anything; instead, pray about everything. Tell God what you need, and thank him for all he has done" (Philippians 4:6, NLT).

Don't worry. Instead, pray. Tell God what you need, *"and thank him for all he has done."*

Do you see a pattern here? Thanksgiving is all over Scripture. Do you know why we are commanded to give thanks to God? It is because God is attached to thanksgiving. He loves it and blesses it when He receives it. It is that important to Him. How do we know that God is attached to thanksgiving? The testimony of Scripture is overwhelming.

Thanksgiving is the sacrifice that God desires

"O my people, listen as I speak. Here are my charges against you, O Israel: I am God, your God! [8] I have no complaint about your sacrifices or the burnt offerings you constantly offer. [9] But I do not need the bulls from your barns or the goats from your pens. [10] For all the animals of the forest are mine, and I own the cattle on a thousand hills. [11] I know every bird on the mountains, and all the animals of the field are mine. [12] If I were hungry, I would not tell you, for all the world is mine and everything in it. [13] Do I eat the meat of bulls? Do I drink the blood

*of goats? ¹⁴ **Make thankfulness your sacrifice to God**, and keep the vows you made to the Most High.¹⁵ Then call on me when you are in trouble, and I will rescue you, and you will give me glory"* (Psalm 50:7-13, NLT, emphasis mine).

He tells them, *"I'm okay with what you are offering to Me, but I don't really need these things. What I really want and what I really need is you making thankfulness your sacrifice to Me."* He says to them that this is the sacrifice that He really wants. Think about that. God is asking for and begging for His people to return thanks to Him. Did you catch what happens when the sacrifice of thanksgiving is given to God? It's one of the ways we know that God is attached to thanksgiving. *"Then call on me when you are in trouble, and I will rescue you, and you will give me glory"* (Psalm 50:15, NLT).

God is moved when we give thanks

He says, *"Make thanksgiving your offering, THEN call on me, and I will rescue you..."* Why will He be quick to come to the rescue? Because God is clearly attached to thanksgiving, and He is moved by it. He has no other choice but to act on your behalf when thanksgiving is given. Look at verse 23 of that same passage.

"But giving thanks is a sacrifice that truly honors me" (Psalm 50:23a, NLT).

Understand, God loves receiving thanks, and He is motivated to act when it is given. It is that important to Him. Not only do we know that God is attached to thanksgiving because He is moved by it when it is given, we also know this important point:

He is grieved and angered when He doesn't receive it

Does it surprise you to know that God is angry when He doesn't receive your thanks? What happened when the children of Israel were wandering in the desert before they reached the Promised Land? They were complaining against God. They were demanding different food and demanding to go back to slavery in Egypt, and it kindled God's wrath against them.

Psalm 106 captures it like this, *"They grumbled in their tents."* It's another way of saying that they refused to thank the Lord.

Think about your own children for one second. You do for them and do for them, and what little thing do you want in return? *"Thank you."* When you don't get it, what do you demand from them? What are you offended by when they don't respond in the right way? God feels the same way.

"But God shows his anger from heaven against all sinful, wicked people who suppress the truth by their wickedness. ¹⁹ They know the truth about God because he has made it obvious to them. ²⁰ For ever since the world was created, people have seen the earth and sky. Through everything God made, they can clearly see his invisible qualities—his eternal power and divine nature. So they have no excuse for not knowing God. ²¹ Yes, they knew God, but they wouldn't worship him as God or even **give him thanks**. *And they began to think up foolish ideas of what God was like. As a result, their minds became dark and confused"* (Romans 1:18-21, NLT, emphasis mine).

God's judgement and wrath is currently being poured out on the world, in Paul's day and in our day, because humanity *"wouldn't worship Him as God or even give Him thanks."* Don't miss this. God equates thanksgiving as worship, and He grieves and is angered when He doesn't get it. Remember in the New Testament when Jesus healed the 10 lepers? How many came back to say, *"Thank you?"* One. And Jesus notices.

Jesus asked, "Didn't I heal ten men? Where are the other nine? ¹⁸ Has no one returned to give glory to God except this foreigner?" (Luke 17:17-18, NLT).

Jesus asks three rapid questions, each one expressing the hurt that was in His heart.

"Didn't I heal 10 men?"

"Where are the other 9?"

"Has no one returned to give glory to God, except this one man who's not even from the house of Israel?"

Why does Luke tell this story? Was it to demonstrate the miraculous healing power of Jesus that was done without physical touch and only by His spoken word? Perhaps. Is it given to show just how far down Jesus will go to save the very least person on the planet? That is how these people would have viewed a Samaritan. Of course. But do you know why I think this story is mentioned? The primary reason for the story is to show just how much Jesus cares about returning thanks to Him, and how it affects Him when He does not receive it.

He receives glory when we give Him thanks

I want to point you to a Scripture that explains this really well. Notice what Paul tells the Corinthian believers.

"We know that God, who raised the Lord Jesus, will also raise us with Jesus and present us to himself together with you. ¹⁵ All of this is for your benefit. And as God's grace reaches more and more people, there will be great thanksgiving, and God will receive more and more glory" (2 Corinthians 4:14-15, NLT).

Did you catch that? As more and more people come to Christ and receive the grace of the Lord, there will be great thanksgiving! What happens when great thanksgiving is given to God? God receives more and more glory. This means that every person who comes to Christ is converted from being a worshipper of this world, to becoming a worshipper of God, overflowing with thankfulness. When people don't come to Christ, and when God's people don't help the people of this world find Jesus, we rob God of the great glory that is due His name in the form of thanksgiving!

Imagine Jesus making a secret appearance on this earth. It's in a 100,000 seat stadium. You are so excited, yet when you get there, you notice that only 1,500 people have come to see Jesus. You quickly think to yourself, *"This is not right! He deserves the worship of the entire world! (And He does). Why aren't more people here?"* We should all then think to ourselves, *"How does God feel about this?"*

The reason why we tell people the Good News about Christ is so that we can gather an army of people to stop worshipping themselves, and the things of this world, so that they can erupt in a magnanimous chorus of praise and thanksgiving to God, for all eternity who is worthy! When we don't do this, **WE ROB GOD OF RECEIVING GLORY.**

Do you know that is exactly what evangelism is? It is turning people from worshipping themselves to worshipping God. That is what every person is designed for: To worship the Lord with all that we are, and give Him thanks. This is why the Apostle Paul says in the very next verse:

"That is why we never give up" (2 Corinthians 4:16a, NLT).

The ultimate reason to never give up is so that people from every tribe, language, people and nation can come under the authoritative rule and reign of Christ and His kingdom, and give Him thanks so that He can receive more and more glory!

This is what God wants. This is what God commands. This is what He loves to receive. This is what moves Him to action. This is what grieves Him when He doesn't receive it. This is what gives Him glory. This is to what He is attached. Thanksgiving. May it always be on our lips towards God, and may it be our goal to have it on the lips of everyone that we come in contact with.

Chapter 10

Attached To Praise

I love to give praise to God. There's something that just feels right every time I engage in that endeavor. I love to quiet myself before the God of the universe and just offer Him praise. I praise Him through song, and I praise Him by just telling Him how great and awesome He is. This kind of overflow of praise should mark every child of God. Do you know that all throughout Scripture, God commands creation to praise Him?

"Sing praises to God and to his name! Sing loud praises to him who rides the clouds. His name is the Lord—rejoice in his presence!" (Psalm 68:4, NLT).

"Praise the Lord, all you nations. Praise him, all you people of the earth" (Psalm 117:1, NLT).

Every person on earth is commanded to praise the Lord, but it's not just limited to people. Everything above the earth, in the earth and below the earth is commanded to praise the Lord as well.

"Praise the Lord. Praise the Lord from the heavens;
   praise him in the heights above.

^{2} *Praise him, all his angels;*
  praise him, all his heavenly hosts.
^{3} *Praise him, sun and moon;*
  praise him, all you shining stars.
^{4} *Praise him, you highest heavens*
  and you waters above the skies.

^{5} *Let them praise the name of the Lord,*
  for at his command they were created,
^{6} *and he established them for ever and ever—*
  he issued a decree that will never pass away.

^{7} *Praise the Lord from the earth,*
  you great sea creatures and all ocean depths,
^{8} *lightning and hail, snow and clouds,*
  stormy winds that do his bidding,
^{9} *you mountains and all hills,*
  fruit trees and all cedars,
^{10} *wild animals and all cattle,*
  small creatures and flying birds,
^{11} *kings of the earth and all nations,*
  you princes and all rulers on earth,
^{12} *young men and women,*
  old men and children.

^{13} *Let them praise the name of the Lord,*
  for his name alone is exalted;
  his splendor is above the earth and the heavens.
^{14} *And he has raised up for his people a horn,*
  the praise of all his faithful servants,
  of Israel, the people close to his heart.

Praise the Lord" (Psalm 148, NIV).

Praise Him, birds! Praise Him, mountains! Praise Him, trees and sun, moon and stars! Let everything bring praise to the *"horn"* that He has raised up, the Lord Jesus Christ!

"Shout for joy to God, all the earth!
² *Sing the glory of his name;*
  make his praise glorious.
³ *Say to God, "How awesome are your deeds!*
  So great is your power
  that your enemies cringe before you.
⁴ *All the earth bows down to you;*
  they sing praise to you,
  they sing the praises of your name" (Psalm 66:1-4, NIV).

Shout! Sing! Say! There it is again. All creation and everything on the earth is commanded to sing praises to God.

"Praise the Lord! Praise God in his sanctuary;
  praise him in his mighty heaven!
² *Praise him for his mighty works;*
  praise his unequaled greatness!
³ *Praise him with a blast of the ram's horn;*
  praise him with the lyre and harp!
⁴ *Praise him with the tambourine and dancing;*
  praise him with strings and flutes!
⁵ *Praise him with a clash of cymbals;*
  praise him with loud clanging cymbals.
⁶ *Let everything that breathes sing praises to the Lord!*

Praise the Lord!" (Psalm 150, NLT).

Praise Him everywhere and in every way with everything! Let everything that has breath praise the Lord!

When Jesus was entering Jerusalem on what we celebrate as Palm Sunday, the people began shouting praise to God for all the wonderful miracles they had seen Him do, but some of the Pharisees in the crowd didn't like what was happening and asked Jesus to rebuke His followers for ascribing to Him Psalm 118 and Psalm 148. Notice what Jesus tells the Pharisees:

He replied, "If they kept quiet, the stones along the road would burst into cheers!" (Luke 19:40, NLT).

He says this because He knows that everything in all creation is made to praise the Lord. God designed it and us to function this way. What does it mean to praise the Lord? When the Bible says, *"Let everything that has breath praise the Lord,"* what does that mean?

There are three Hebrew words in the Bible that are translated as praise. One is *"yadah,"* which means *"praise or give thanks or confess."* Another one is *"zamar,"* which means *"sing praise."*

The third one is *"halal,"* (which is the root word for hallelujah), which means *"to praise, honor, or commend."*

We can summarize these three in this way:

To praise is to express adoration or approval

We do that with our lips and with our hearts, and we are to continually offer up a sacrifice of praise to God. Do you know that David, in the Old Testament, appointed certain Levites in the Temple to offer up praise to God?

"David also appointed Heman, Jeduthun, and the others chosen by name to give thanks to the Lord, for "his faithful love endures forever." ⁴² They used their trumpets, cymbals, and other instruments to accompany their songs of praise to God. And the sons of Jeduthun were appointed as gatekeepers" (1 Chron 16:41-42, NLT).

Look at 1 Chronicles 23 as it gives more detail about David's appointed musicians.

"Another 4,000 will work as gatekeepers, and 4,000 will praise the Lord with the musical instruments I have made" (1 Chronicles 23:5, NLT).

Skip down to verse 30 of that same chapter and notice what it says further about these men.

"And each morning and evening they stood before the Lord to sing songs of thanks and praise to him" (1 Chronicles 23:30, NLT).

Why would David appoint 4,000 Levites to praise the Lord, every morning and every evening? Why would he do that? Because he knew that praise influences the Almighty, and He knew that God is attached to praise. This is why all creation is commanded to praise the Lord. He commands it because He is attached to it.

Look at Ephesians 5 and notice what it says.

"Don't be drunk with wine, because that will ruin your life. Instead, be filled with the Holy Spirit, 19 singing psalms and hymns and spiritual songs among yourselves, and making music to the Lord in your hearts" (Ephesians 5:18-19, NLT).

What happens when we are filled with the Holy Spirit? The text says that we will overflow with praise. The Holy Spirit leads us to this place. Why? Because God is attached to praise.

What does it mean that God is attached to praise? What happens when praise is given to Him? Are you ready? Because He is attached to it, it means that He's obligated to do things when praise is given to Him. Obligated. Notice clearly.

Praise leads to presence

Remember what happened when Solomon dedicated the Temple?

"Then the priests left the Holy Place. All the priests who were present had purified themselves, whether or not they were on duty that day. 12 And the Levites who were musicians—Asaph, Heman, Jeduthun, and all their sons and brothers—were dressed in fine linen robes and stood at the east side of the altar playing cymbals, lyres, and harps. They were joined by 120 priests who were playing trumpets. 13 The trumpeters and singers performed together in unison to praise and give thanks to the Lord. Accompanied by trumpets, cymbals, and

other instruments, they raised their voices and praised the Lord with these words:

"He is good!
  His faithful love endures forever!"

At that moment a thick cloud filled the Temple of the Lord. ¹⁴ *The priests could not continue their service because of the cloud, for the glorious presence of the Lord filled the Temple of God"* (2 Chronicles 5:11-14, NLT).

The Bible says that praise was given and *"at that moment"* the presence of the Lord came. Was that by coincidence? Of course not! God responds to praise, so much so that the priests were unable to continue their work in the Temple because the presence of the Lord among them was so overwhelming.

The way to experience the presence of God and to draw near to the Lord is to praise Him, recognizing that He is our Creator, that He is our joy, that He is our satisfaction, and that He is our God. It is giving to Him the glory and honor that is due His name. God loves it when we praise Him and sing to Him, and He draws near when it is given.

"Shout with joy to the Lord, all the earth!
²   *Worship the Lord with gladness.*
  Come before him, singing with joy.
³ *Acknowledge that the Lord is God!*
  He made us, and we are his.
  We are his people, the sheep of his pasture.
⁴ *Enter his gates with thanksgiving;*
  go into his courts with praise.
  Give thanks to him and praise his name" (Psalm 100:1-4, NLT).

I've often wondered about this passage. Is it that we are to go into His presence with thanksgiving and praise, or could it be that His presence is opened to us, once we give Him the sacrifice of thanksgiving and praise? Enter with thanksgiving. Go into His presence with praise.

Perhaps this is why David commanded praise be given to God every morning and every evening.

"Yet you are holy, enthroned on the praises of Israel" (Psalm 22:3, NLT).

God is enthroned on the praises of His people. He inhabits those praises. When we praise, I firmly believe that His presence is revealed. Look at what is happening right now in Heaven.

"And when he took the scroll, the four living beings and the twenty-four elders fell down before the Lamb. Each one had a harp, and they held gold bowls filled with incense, which are the prayers of God's people. ⁹ And they sang a new song with these words:

"You are worthy to take the scroll
and break its seals and open it.
For you were slaughtered, and your blood has ransomed people for God from every tribe and language and people and nation.
¹⁰ And you have caused them to become
a Kingdom of priests for our God.
And they will reign on the earth."

¹¹ Then I looked again, and I heard the voices of thousands and millions of angels around the throne and of the living beings and the elders. ¹² And they sang in a mighty chorus:

"Worthy is the Lamb who was slaughtered—
to receive power and riches
and wisdom and strength
and honor and glory and blessing."

¹³ And then I heard every creature in heaven and on earth and under the earth and in the sea. They sang:

"Blessing and honor and glory and power
belong to the one sitting on the throne
and to the Lamb forever and ever."

14 And the four living beings said, "Amen!" And the twenty-four elders fell down and worshiped the Lamb" (Revelation 5:8-11, NLT).

This has been happening, is currently happening, and will forever happen in the presence of God. Heaven is a place of unending praise offered to God who is present and who is worthy. Praise leads to the throne room of God. Because He is attached to it and moved by it, make it a habit in your life to offer Him continual praise.

Praise leads to power

Look at Acts 16 and the story of Paul and Silas in jail.

"So the jailer put them into the inner dungeon and clamped their feet in the stocks. 25 Around midnight Paul and Silas were praying and singing hymns to God, and the other prisoners were listening. 26 Suddenly, there was a massive earthquake, and the prison was shaken to its foundations. All the doors immediately flew open, and the chains of every prisoner fell off!" (Acts 16:24-26 (NLT).

Around midnight, Paul and Silas were praying and singing hymns to God, and what happened when they began praising God? God showed up in their life in powerful way. Is that by some random chance? No. They prayed and praised God through song, and God showed up in power, and God will do the same in your circumstances because He has attached Himself to the praises of His people.

Remember when the children of Israel marched around Jericho? They marched around the city once a day for six days. On the seventh day they walked around the city seven times. Every time they walked they carried with them the Ark of the Covenant, as the priests marched ahead of the Ark blowing a ram's horn. Notice what happens after the seventh trip around the city on the seventh day.

"When the people heard the sound of the rams' horns, they shouted as loud as they could. Suddenly, the walls of Jericho collapsed, and the Israelites charged straight into the town and captured it" (Joshua

6:20, NLT).

The walls fell because of shouts of praise. They didn't have to lift a finger to move the wall. They obeyed the Lord, and He did all the work. Power comes forth when praise is given to God.

Let me show you one other example. Look at 2 Chronicles 20. In this chapter, King Jehoshaphat and the people of Israel were being attacked by three armies. These armies were coming to wipe out the people of God. Notice how Jehoshaphat responds to this crisis.

"Then King Jehoshaphat bowed low with his face to the ground. And all the people of Judah and Jerusalem did the same, worshiping the Lord. ¹⁹ Then the Levites from the clans of Kohath and Korah stood to praise the Lord, the God of Israel, with a very loud shout. ²⁰ Early the next morning the army of Judah went out into the wilderness of Tekoa. On the way Jehoshaphat stopped and said, "Listen to me, all you people of Judah and Jerusalem! Believe in the Lord your God, and you will be able to stand firm. Believe in his prophets, and you will succeed." ²¹ After consulting the people, the king appointed singers to walk ahead of the army, singing to the Lord and praising him for his holy splendor. This is what they sang:

"Give thanks to the Lord;
  his faithful love endures forever!"

²² **At the very moment they began to sing and give praise**, *the Lord caused the armies of Ammon, Moab, and Mount Seir to start fighting among themselves. ²³ The armies of Moab and Ammon turned against their allies from Mount Seir and killed every one of them. After they had destroyed the army of Seir, they began attacking each other. ²⁴ So when the army of Judah arrived at the lookout point in the wilderness, all they saw were dead bodies lying on the ground as far as they could see. Not a single one of the enemy had escaped"* (2 Chronicles 20:18-24, NLT, emphasis mine).

When did God act on their behalf? *"At the very moment they began to sing and give praise."* Now can you see that this is a pattern in God's economy? Praise leads to power and God showing up large in your life and in your circumstances. If you are desperate to see the Lord work or if you are in a defeated mindset, set your mind to praise the Lord, ascribing to Him the worship due His name.

Praise leads to position

What do I mean by this? I mean the position of spiritual authority over the enemy. I believe that once we begin to praise the Lord, the devil flees.

"Through the praise of children and infants you have established a stronghold against your enemies, to silence the foe and the avenger" (Psalm 8:2, NIV).

Remember when David, when he was much younger, was sent to the palace to live with Saul?

David had great music ability and great song writing ability, and Saul knew that. Notice how God used David's musical ability in Saul's life at that time.

"And whenever the tormenting spirit from God troubled Saul, David would play the harp. Then Saul would feel better, and the tormenting spirit would go away" (1 Samuel 16:23, NLT).

Simply put, the devil hates it when we sing to God and praise Him, and I believe that it repels Him when we do it. Why? He knows that our eyes are off of our circumstances and are squarely on the Lord. It is the devil who wants to keep our eyes on our circumstances, but the moment we begin to praise the Lord, no matter the circumstances, the devil leaves. He also knows that when praise is given to the Lord, the Lord draws near.

Praise leads to presence. If you want to experience the nearness of God, begin singing His praises. Praise leads to power. God moves on behalf of the people who choose to praise Him. I do not fully understand how that works, but I know that the Lord works when His people praise Him. Praise also leads to position over the enemy. The devil hates it when we praise God and he flees when it begins. Let me close with one last verse.

"Therefore, let us offer through Jesus a continual sacrifice of praise to God, proclaiming our allegiance to his name" (Hebrews 13:15, NLT).

As we are filled with the Holy Spirit, He will lead us in a continual offering of praise to God. May this be the case, in all of our lives, as we submit to His authority and continually offer ourselves to Him.

Chapter 11

Attached To Faith

During my first trip to Africa, I went with an organization that took our team on safari in Kenya the last two days we were there. While we were eating a sack lunch in the jeep, we got to witness one of the seven natural wonders in the world—the great migration.

Wildebeests were crossing the Masai Mara River from the Serengeti to the Masai Mara. Some people go to Africa to see this but miss it. We got to see it within 30 minutes of arriving while eating a sack lunch. Isn't that great?

Now, the reason why it's sometimes a difficult event to witness is because the wildebeests don't always cooperate. Thousands gather and cluster at the water's edge. They know that danger is lurking in those waters in the form of hungry crocodiles, and the wildebeests are all waiting for one thing to happen; for one of them to take the lead. They all wait for one animal in their group to jump into the water, and once one does, they all follow.

How does this relate to us as believers? This is what God is wanting from us. Faith. To courageously trust Him and step into the water no matter who else does. There is an amazing verse in Hebrews 11.

*"And without faith it is **impossible** to please God, because anyone who comes to him must believe that he exists and that he rewards those who earnestly seek him"* (Hebrews 11:6, NIV, emphasis mine).

Did you notice the wording in the verse? It doesn't say, *"Improbable."* It doesn't say, *"Hard."* It doesn't even say, *"Unlikely."* It says *"Impossible."* *"Without faith it is impossible to please God."* If that is the case, what should that immediately tell you about God? God is attached to faith! He's attached to it, and before He moves or acts or does, God mandates faith.

In other words, He requires that it be present before anything else can be moved forward. This is exactly how God operates in our lives today. Did you know that? God mandates that faith be present. Think about salvation. What happens to you when you put your faith and trust in Jesus? What all do you have access to now?

Heaven,

Indwelled with the Holy Spirit,

Right with God,

Every spiritual blessing given to us in Christ,

Adopted into the family of God,

Sons and daughters of the reigning King,

All principalities and powers under our feet,

Victorious in Christ,

No longer guilty,

No longer living in fear,

No longer slaves, and the list could go on and on!

None of that is accessible until you demonstrate faith and put your trust in the plan that God has made. That plan is Jesus Christ.

"If you declare with your mouth, "Jesus is Lord," and believe in your heart that God raised him from the dead, you will be saved. ¹⁰ For it is with your heart that you believe and are justified, and it is with your mouth that you profess your faith and are saved" (Romans 10:9-10, NIV).

Until faith in Christ is present, you cannot be saved. That's just how much God has attached Himself to it.

Some of you are thinking to yourself even at this very moment, *"God, why don't you show up in my life?"* or *"God why don't I see you working?"* or *"Why don't I see the blessing of God in my life,"* and God emphatically says, *"I can't! Faith must be present in order for Me to work!"*

Every time you set out to do something, do it with the mindset that God mandates faith. He's attached to it, and He will not work until you trust Him to put your feet in the water just like the lead wildebeest. Every person in the Bible who encountered God understood this about God.

Moses

When Moses and the children of Israel were about to cross the Red Sea, God doesn't just part the waters for them. What does He tell Moses? *"Stretch out your staff."* Once Moses obeys in faith, God opens up the sea into dry ground.

Naaman

2 Kings 5 talks about Naaman, the Captain of the Armies of Syria, who had leprosy. He goes to Elisha the Prophet, and Elisha does not come out to meet him. He simply sends word to Naaman to wash seven times in the Jordan River, and then he would be healed.

What does Naaman do at this point? Naaman gets angry and refuses to do such a silly thing but his servants urged him to obey. When he finally relents and demonstrates faith in what Elijah asks him to do, his skin is restored, and he finds out that the God of Israel is the One True God. Look up the story. Before God healed him, Naaman had to demonstrate faith.

The Boy With Fish and Bread

Remember that boy? The boy in John chapter 6 that had five loaves of bread and two fish? He demonstrated faith by giving his lunch to Jesus, and Jesus feeds an estimated 15,000 people with much left over. The lunch had to be given in faith before the miracle could take place.

Peter

Peter walked on the water but first he had to demonstrate faith by getting out of the boat.

In order to experience God's power, He requires that faith be present. In order for salvation or transformation or the supernatural to take place, God requires that we obediently take the first step of faith.

Let me show you a great example of this. It's found in Joshua chapter 3. In Joshua 3, Moses has died, and Joshua is now their leader. At this time, God is about to lead the children of Israel from the wilderness, into the Promised Land. Here they are in this moment. They arrive at the banks of the Jordan River, and when they arrive, God gives them specific instructions.

"Now choose twelve men from the tribes of Israel, one from each tribe. 13 The priests will carry the Ark of the Lord, the Lord of all the earth. As soon as their feet touch the water, the flow of water will be cut off upstream, and the river will stand up like a wall." 14 So the people left their camp to cross the Jordan, and the priests who were carrying the Ark of the Covenant went ahead of them. 15 It was the harvest season, and the Jordan was overflowing its banks. But as soon as the feet of the priests who were carrying the Ark touched the water at the river's

edge, ¹⁶the water above that point began backing up a great distance away at a town called Adam, which is near Zarethan. And the water below that point flowed on to the Dead Sea until the riverbed was dry. Then all the people crossed over near the town of Jericho.

¹⁷Meanwhile, the priests who were carrying the Ark of the Lord's Covenant stood on dry ground in the middle of the riverbed as the people passed by. They waited there until the whole nation of Israel had crossed the Jordan on dry ground (Joshua 3:12-17, NLT).

I want you to picture this scene in your mind. Moses, their leader, has just died, and now they are inheriting a new leader, Joshua. They are coming from wandering in the wilderness with nothing but the Ark of God, and they are about to cross over into the Promised land, the land that they have been hearing about ever since they left Egypt.

What did the Ark of the Covenant symbolize? It symbolized the presence, authority, and power of God. It symbolized that the *"Lord of all the earth"* was with them and had not abandoned them. But, understand, it was not enough for them to have the Ark with them. The water did not move simply because they had the Ark. No, the water does not move until they obediently put their feet in the water, demonstrating faith in what God told them to do.

I want you to think about this: God could have easily parted the water for them as they approached, but God required that they obediently demonstrate faith in Him. This is how He works, and this is why He mandates it. He is attached to faith and requires that it be present before He can work.

Until the priests obediently put their feet in the water, just like God told them to do, the water did not move, and it was not going to move until faith was present. Some of you, in all honesty, are violating this understanding of faith. You're trying to earn your way to God without coming to Jesus, the Way, the Truth and the Life.

For some of you, God has asked you to surrender your finances to Him and you just won't do it. Understand, there is no greater joy than giving to Jesus all that you have, so that He can do with you all that He wants.

For some of you, God is asking you to surrender your marriage to Him, to let Him, instead of you, control it. He's asking that you to do the same with your kids. Maybe He's asking you to give up a relationship in your life that's not right, and you have yet to trust Him with that. Whatever it is, by faith, surrender that to Him. You say, *"Pastor Matt, how can I do that?"* Let me give you a couple of things.

Step out of your trust and into the water of His trust

Faith really comes down to this issue: Either you trust yourself or you trust God. Either you trust God with your salvation, or you trust yourself and your good works. Either you trust God with your finances, or you trust God who owns everything. See what I mean? A lack of faith is a lack of trust in the Lord, and faith requires that you trust Him.

There is this story about a man who is lost in the desert and dying of thirst. He stumbles upon an old shack where he finds an old, rusty water pump. Next to the pump was a full jug of water with a note: *"Prime the pump with all the water in this jug. Be sure to fill the jug again before you leave."*

Stop right there. This man is dying of thirst, and he's holding fresh, clean, water in his hand. What would you do? Would you drink it, or would you, by faith, obey the instructions and pour all of the water in the jug into the pump?

The man decided to analyze the situation a little further. He pumped the handle of the pump up and down to see if anything would come out before pouring all of the water into the pump. Nothing happened. Now, he's suddenly faced with a huge decision. *"Drink what I have in my hand or demonstrate faith."*

He decides to pour all of the water into the pump. He pumps. Nothing. He pumps again. Nothing. He pumps a little more, a trickle. He keeps pumping, and then the water flows. When that happens, he drinks to his fulfillment. When he finished filling his belly, he then filled the jug back up and added a little post script to the note: *"Believe me it really works; you have to give it all away before you can get anything back."* The same is true with faith in God.

Step out of your control and into the water of His control

Don't you know that control is an illusion? It is. How much can you really control? I would much rather abandon myself to the control of the Maker of Heaven and earth than abandon myself to my own control. Wouldn't you? That's faith, and that's what God requires, and here's what you find on the other side of faith: Him! You find that the Lord of all the earth is attached to faith!

That's what Moses found out. That's what Naaman found out. That's what the boy who gave his small lunch away found out. That's what Peter found out, and that's what the priests carrying the Ark found out. They found the Lord Almighty when they demonstrated faith, and that is what we will find as well. When faith is present, we find the Lord, who is attached to faith.

When you demonstrate faith in Him, when you let go of yourself, your trust and your control, and when you, by faith, give that to Him, you find Him and all that He is and all that He has, which is all that we ever need. God lives on the other side of faith. There is no other way to get to Him until you demonstrate faith. He's attached to it. This is why He requires it.

Stop for one second in this moment and ask yourself, *"In what area of my life do I need to exhibit faith?"*

Just like the man, who was dying of thirst in the desert, said after the water flowed and he drank to his hearts content, *"Believe me it really works; you have to give it all away before you can get anything back,"* this is what we need to understand about God. God dwells in the land of faith, and He works mightily through those who give everything over to Him by faith. See Him through that lens from now on.

Chapter 12

Attached To Desperation

Do you know what resonates with God? Desperation. God is near desperate people. He's attached to them. The problem with most people, however, is that they don't know how desperate they really are. The thing about desperation is that it forces you to decide. Either to harden your heart or humble your heart. To rebel or bow. The latter forces you to become real and honest with God. The former causes you to blame everyone but yourself.

Jesus taught desperation

*"The Kingdom of Heaven is like a treasure that a man discovered hidden in a field. In his excitement, he hid it again and **sold every-thing he owned** to get enough money to buy the field. ⁴⁵"Again, the Kingdom of Heaven is like a merchant on the lookout for choice pearls. ⁴⁶ When he discovered a pearl of great value, **he sold everything he owned** and bought it!"* (Matthew 13:44-46 NLT; emphasis mine).

This is to what Jesus compares salvation—selling everything you have in order to get it. It's not casual. It's not indifferent. It's desperate.

"A large crowd was following Jesus. He turned around and said to them, ²⁶ "If you want to be my disciple, you must hate everyone else

*by comparison—your father and mother, wife and children, brothers and sisters—yes, even your own life. Otherwise, **you cannot be my disciple**. ²⁷ And if you do not carry your own cross and follow me, **you cannot be my disciple***" (Luke 14:25-27 NLT; emphasis mine).

In the Sermon on the Mount, The Beatitudes in Matthew 5 are all about spiritual desperation. It is a chronology of salvation and what happens to a person when they are transformed from the inside out by Jesus, and it starts with desperation. *"Blessed are the poor in spirit..."* Not the proud in spirit.

Jesus was always trying to get His disciples to the place of desperation. Before he fed the 5,000 men (not counting women and children), he first asked his disciples to feed the crowd. They exclaimed, *"Impossible! "We only have a few loaves of bread and a few fish."* But what Jesus was trying to teach them is that they didn't even need that. All they needed was Him.

Jesus lived desperation

He lived it in the Garden of Gethsemane.

Then Jesus went with them to the olive grove called Gethsemane, and he said, "Sit here while I go over there to pray." ³⁷ He took Peter and Zebedee's two sons, James and John, and he became anguished and distressed. ³⁸ He told them, "My soul is crushed with grief to the point of death. Stay here and keep watch with me." ³⁹ He went on a little farther and bowed with his face to the ground, praying, "My Father! If it is possible, let this cup of suffering be taken away from me. Yet I want your will to be done, not mine" (Matthew 26:36-39 NLT).

Jesus said to the Father, *"If there's any other way, let it be done. But, Father, it's not what I want. I will do whatever you ask of Me."* Jesus experienced desperation while on this earth.

Jesus Loved Desperate People

Jesus encountered all different kinds of people. He encountered those who were proud and self-righteous, and He encountered those who wanted Him for nothing more than personal gain. I sometimes see myself in all of these people. He became angry at the proud and self-righteous people. Look at what he said to the Pharisees in front of his disciples and the crowds standing by.

"What sorrow awaits you teachers of religious law and you Pharisees. Hypocrites! For you are so careful to clean the outside of the cup and the dish, but inside you are filthy—full of greed and self-indulgence! ²⁶ You blind Pharisee! First wash the inside of the cup and the dish, and then the outside will become clean, too. ²⁷ "What sorrow awaits you teachers of religious law and you Pharisees. Hypocrites! For you are like whitewashed tombs—beautiful on the outside but filled on the inside with dead people's bones and all sorts of impurity. ²⁸ Outwardly you look like righteous people, but inwardly your hearts are filled with hypocrisy and lawlessness" (Matthew 23:25-28 NLT).

To those looking out for personal gain on the coattails of Jesus, he ran away from them. Here's the scene right after he feeds the five thousand:

*"When the people saw him do this miraculous sign, they exclaimed, "Surely, he is the Prophet we have been expecting!" ¹⁵When Jesus saw that they were ready to force him to be their king, **he slipped away into the hills by himself**"* (John 6:14-15 NLT; emphasis mine).

But the desperate—he couldn't get enough of because He's attached to them. Look at his encounter with the leprous man.

*In one of the villages, Jesus met a man with an advanced case of leprosy. When the man saw Jesus, he **bowed** with his face to the ground, **begging** to be healed. "Lord," he said, "if you are willing, you can heal me and make me clean." ¹³ Jesus reached out and touched him. "I am willing," he said. "Be healed!" And instantly the leprosy disappeared* (Luke 5:12-13 NLT; emphasis mine).

I love that! He bowed and he begged for Jesus to heal him. He did the same thing for a man named Jairus.

*"On the other side of the lake the crowds welcomed Jesus, because they had been waiting for him. ⁴¹ Then a man named Jairus, a leader of the local synagogue, came and **fell** at Jesus' feet, **pleading** with him to come home with him. ⁴² His only daughter, who was about twelve years old, was dying. As Jesus went with him, he was surrounded by the crowds"* (Luke 8:40-42 NLT; emphasis mine).

Jairus was Jewish clergy—the leader of the local synagogue. This was an elected position. It would have been one of the most revered positions in the Jewish community. Do you think the *"crowd"* looked favorably upon him for coming to Jesus and coming to Him like that? He was supposed to be dignified and upstanding.

He's also Jewish establishment. How did the Jewish leadership view Jesus at this time? The Chief Council in Jerusalem was already infuriated with Jesus and His teaching. By this time in Jesus' ministry, He is on every *"unapproved"* list and on notice with every synagogue ruler. Yet, Jairus fell down and kissed the feet of Jesus.

He was literally laying his reputation in the community on the line. If Jesus was unable to heal, his career is over. But, Jairus didn't care what people thought about him or what he thought about Jesus at that point. All he knew was that he was desperate, and that he needed help fast. He bursts through the crowd and begs for help.

Why is he coming? His only daughter is dying. Here you have a parent in peril, and there's nothing like it. If you are a parent, you know what I'm talking about. When you are charged with the responsibility to care for and defend a little life, there's nothing you won't do when something happens. You become desperate very fast, just like the woman with the issue of blood:

A woman in the crowd had suffered for twelve years with constant bleeding, (she had spent everything she had on doctors) and she could find no cure. ⁴⁴ Coming up behind Jesus, she touched the fringe of his robe. Immediately, the bleeding stopped. ⁴⁵ *"Who touched me?" Jesus asked. Everyone denied it, and Peter said, "Master, this whole crowd is pressing up against you."* ⁴⁶ *But Jesus said, "Someone deliberately touched me, for I felt healing power go out from me."* ⁴⁷ *When the woman realized that she could not stay hidden, she began to tremble and fell to her knees in front of him. The whole crowd heard her explain why she had touched him and that she had been immediately healed.* ⁴⁸*"Daughter," he said to her, "your faith has made you well. Go in peace"* (Luke 8:43-48 NLT).

This sick woman was hopeless. Let me explain. There were three types of uncleanness that were serious enough to give a person *"outcast"* status. Leprosy, bodily discharge, and contact with the dead. The discharge from which she suffered, according to Leviticus 15 automatically made her perpetually unclean. This means that:

She would have been excluded from the synagogue and the Temple. Maybe even Jairus had to push her out. If she were married, she would have likely been divorced because of this issue. If she had children, she would have been unable to hug them for fear of making them unclean.

Anything she touched, sat on, or laid on would now be considered *"unclean."* Whoever or whatever touched her would have to be washed, clothes changed, and remain *"unclean"* until evening. Pastor and author Chuck Swindoll says this about her condition.

"She would have her eyes downcast as you pass her by. She is self-conscious, ashamed and afraid. She reads the condescension in your eyes. She fears the indifference of your shoulder turned coldly against her. But most of all, she fears the judgment you bring down on her life; that her illness is the direct result of some personal sin. And with a bleeding uterus, anyone could guess what kind of sin it was." [1]

Her private world was constantly made public and thrown in her face. She had spent everything she had on doctors, and there was no cure in sight. She knew that she had to get to Jesus. She was desperate. As she fought her way through the crowd, she grabbed hold of Jesus' garment.

This was not out of curiosity but desperation. She knew the risk. To be touched by a menstruating woman would make Jesus ceremonially unclean. To rub shoulders with anyone in the crowd would mean that they, every person she touched, would now be considered unclean. She would be condemned and she knew that. But it was a risk she was willing to take.

When she touched Him, she was immediately healed. Even Jesus was startled by it. *"Who touched me?"* Peter tries to get Jesus to *"assess"* the situation by pointing out the large crowd that was surrounding Him, but Jesus says something, clarifying what he meant. Don't miss this. *"Someone **deliberately** touched me."* That's the key. Deliberate desperation. That's what Jesus is constantly looking for. Jesus healed this woman, and he raised Jairus' daughter back to life again because He loves to rescue desperate people.

Let me give you another example of Jesus being attached to desperation, which is going to require a little explanation. It's the faith of a Phoenician Woman from the area called Tyre, located on the Mediterranean Sea. Her story is found in Matthew 15.

Leaving that place, Jesus withdrew to the region of Tyre and Sidon. *22 A Canaanite woman from that vicinity came to him, crying out, "Lord, Son of David, have mercy on me! My daughter is demon-possessed and suffering terribly." 23 Jesus did not answer a word. So his disciples came to him and urged him, "Send her away, for she keeps crying out after us."*

24 He answered, "I was sent only to the lost sheep of Israel."

25 The woman came and knelt before him. "Lord, help me!" she said.

26 He replied, "It is not right to take the children's bread and toss it to the dogs."

27 "Yes it is, Lord," she said. "Even the dogs eat the crumbs that fall from their master's table."

28 Then Jesus said to her, "Woman, you have great faith! Your request is granted." And her daughter was healed at that moment (Matthew 15:21-28, NIV).

What is this about? Jesus is seemingly ignoring this woman and then likening her to a dog! This doesn't sound very Christ-like and this is coming from the source! What is going on here? Let's ask a few questions about the text. Who is this person searching for Jesus, begging for Him to heal? The text gives us three clues:

She Is a Woman

Why is this significant? In this culture, being a woman is tantamount to being nothing more than a child or an animal, having little to no value.

She Is a Gentile

She's not part of the covenant people, Israel. She is part of Rome, and every good Jew hates Rome.

She Is a Canaanite

This is her religion. She more than likely did not grow up worshipping the God of the Bible, but all the pagan gods of the land.

Usually, three strikes means, *"You're out,"* but she has a crisis in her life. She's desperate. Her daughter is demon possessed and severely tormented. We are not told how old the daughter is, or for how long she has been tormented. We are told only that the condition is bad enough for her to come searching, and screaming and eventually begging at Jesus' feet. Mark's Gospel sheds a little more light on the timing of the story.

"Then Jesus left Galilee and went north to the region of Tyre. He didn't want anyone to know which house he was staying in, but he couldn't keep it a secret" (Mark 7:24, NLT).

Jesus didn't want anyone to know in which VRBO He and His disciples were staying. Jesus is in vacation mode, and He and his disciples have traveled outside of the country to Gentile territory to unplug from the crowds. It's much needed rest, and what a beautiful place in which to unwind, the Mediterranean Sea.

He finds a house that is somewhat tucked away, but the fame of Jesus can't be hidden for long. This woman has heard about Him and has a desperate need in her life. Let's analyze the scene. The Gospel accounts say that this woman was crying out, *"Lord, Son of David, have mercy on me! My daughter is demon possessed and is suffering terribly."*

We don't know exactly where Jesus is at this point. Is He inside the house? I believe he is. Is she shouting out in the open like the two blind men that Jesus encountered on his way out of Jericho? *"Lord, Son of David have mercy on us!"* I believe she is.

Pay attention to what she calls Him in her shouting. *"Lord, Son of David."* She recognizes Him as Lord and recognizes Him as Messiah. *"This is THE One from the lineage of King David,"* a sign that many Jews have missed, but she gets it. She believes Him to be God in the flesh. And, how does Jesus respond?

"Jesus did not answer a word" (Matthew 15:23a, NIV).

Isn't that interesting? Jesus doesn't answer her right away. We are not told why. Again, we don't exactly know where Jesus is at this point, but His disciples do. They find Him, and notice what they ask Him.

So his disciples came to him and urged him, "Send her away, for she keeps crying out after us" (Matthew 15:23b, NIV).

"Please help us. Send her away." Her desperation was wearing them out. The disciples seem to have no compassion whatsoever. I get it. They are worn out and sleep deprived. They've been around crowds non-stop, and they are in vacation mode! Notice what Jesus says to them.

He answered, "I was sent only to the lost sheep of Israel" (Matthew

15:24, NIV).

He reminded his disciples of the system that God had originally set up. God gave salvation to the Jews so that the Jews could give it away to the rest of the world. Instead of doing that and being a light to the nations, they kept it for themselves. Jesus, however, was making them aware of what was supposed to be. Eventually the woman finds her way into the house where Jesus was. Notice the encounter.

The woman came and knelt before him. "Lord, help me!" she said.

[26] *He replied, "It is not right to take the children's bread and toss it to the dogs"* (Matthew 15:25-26 (NIV)

What a tender moment! She kneels before Jesus and directly asks Him, *"Lord, help me."*

Her desperation is in the right spot, but Jesus replies with an unusual response. *"It is not right to take the children's bread and toss it to the dogs."*

Before you get upset, let me take some time here. Jesus uses an analogy. He says that feeding the children takes place over feeding the house-hold puppy. That's the word that is used here. It's not that the puppy is not going to be taken care of or well fed. It's just going to have to wait until the appropriate time. This is point that He was trying to convey to His disciples.

How many of you have a family pet? We have one. She's a little dog named Rosie. How many of you love your pet and take care of your pet? How many of you treat your household pet like a member of the family, or better than the people in your family?

Using this understanding, let me explain what Jesus is saying to this woman. It was not a matter of *"No."* It was a matter of *"Wait."* To para-phrase, He says something like this: *"It's not right to take food off the table that was intended for the children and instead give it to Rosie. The little puppy that you care for is just going to have to wait."*

This is in essence what He's telling her, but she doesn't take *"No"* or *"Wait"* for an answer. Remember, she's desperate. Notice how she replies to Jesus.

"Yes it is, Lord," she said. "Even the dogs eat the crumbs that fall from their master's table" (Matthew 15:27, NIV).

Jesus says, *"It's not right"* and she says, *"Yes it is,"* and she then gives Jesus an analogy of her own! *"Lord, even the puppies hang out under the table, and even sometimes the children drop crumbs either unintentionally or intentionally."*

This happens at our house all the time when Rosie hangs out under our table during dinner time. Here's the brilliance of what she said. She said that she didn't want to take anything away from the children. She didn't want to disrupt the order. She reminded Jesus that He had the power to bless her AT THE SAME TIME! Jesus could accomplish His intended order AND take care of her need as well. She confessed that Jesus only needs *"crumb-sized power"* to meet her need! Notice how Jesus praises her.

Then Jesus said to her, "Woman, you have great faith! Your request is granted." And her daughter was healed at that moment (Matthew 15:28, NIV).

He doesn't say, *"Woman, you are persistent."* He says, *"Woman, you have great faith."* In other words, Jesus was deeply moved by such a powerful, desperate faith in Him. What was it about her faith that amazed Jesus?

She was convinced of who He was

She knew that He was God in the flesh, and she, like Jairus knew that only He could save her daughter.

She wouldn't take "No" for an answer

She could have easily walked away. She had all of these strikes against her. She was not the right religion, color, or creed. She wasn't well received by the disciples. She even had to push through barriers with Jesus. But she would not be denied. She persisted, because she was desperate, and here's what Jesus is wanting everyone to know who hears her story: *"Don't give up! Push through! Come after Me with all that you've got."* He loves it when we come after Him in desperation, and He's moved by it. I want you to consider these three thoughts.

Desperate people don't care that people know they are desperate

For them, it's not about who's watching or what people might say. They're desperate. The only thing that they know is that their need has to be met. How many of us hang back because we're scared of what people might think or say? It's not about desperation for us at that point. It's about pride, and it's about preserving our self-image, but the only opinion that should concern us is God's opinion.

Desperate people want Jesus so badly that they'll do anything to get Him

They don't give up. They don't tire out. They persist and pursue. Like Jairus. Like the woman with the issue of blood. Like the man who sold everything in order to get the treasure. Like the desperate Phoenician woman. It gives God great joy when we pursue Him like this, because when it gets to this point, He knows that He's all we've got and all we want.

Desperate people totally rely on Jesus

Jesus is their only hope. It's not Jesus plus something else. It's Jesus plus nothing else. For Jairus, it wasn't Jesus plus a doctor. For the woman with the issue of blood, it wasn't Jesus plus money. For the Phoeni-cian woman it wasn't Jesus plus a calm, dignified demeanor. No! They pushed through the crowd. They put their reputations on the line. They yelled out, interrupted, and wouldn't take *"No"* for an answer. Why? They truly believed that Jesus was their only hope.

Are you willing to become desperate? It's the only kind of people God accepts. He's attached to them. Desperate people. Let me close with this. Are you familiar with the story, *"Three Feet from Gold?"*

"Darby's uncle had gone West to Colorado during the gold rush days and eventually came across gold ore. In the need of min-ing machinery to dig up more gold, Darby's uncle returned home to Maryland to secure financing for the machinery. While there, he also was able to enlist Darby's help. Once financing was se-cured, Darby and his uncle returned to Colorado to work the mine.

Initially, things were going well. The first remnants of gold they dis-covered were shipped to a smelter and the returns provided a promise that they could have one of Colorado's richest mines. A few more gold discoveries like the first, could clear Darby and his uncle of all their debt and leave them very rich. Needless to say, they were hopeful as they continued to drill.

Then the unbelievable happened. The vein of gold ore they had been successfully drilling just disappeared. Confident they would find more gold Darby and his uncle continued to drill, day after day, with no luck. Every day of drilling drove them both deeper into debt and until finally, they both decided to quit! They sold the drilling machinery to a nearby junkman and returned home.

The junkman wasn't convinced that their mine had no gold, so he hired a mining engineer to get an expert opinion before breaking down all of the drilling machinery to be sold. The engineer's findings were shocking! He found that the vein of gold ore that Darby and his uncle had been seeking, was just three feet from where they had stopped drilling! The junkman decided to continue drilling and that is exactly where the gold was found!" [2]

God loves desperation and is moved by it. Don't quit mining. Don't quit drilling. Don't quit praying. Don't quit coming to God in desperation. He's not threatened by it. He loves it because He's attached to it, and when God calls you a puppy, bark as loudly as you can!

---

[1] Chuck Swindoll, *"The Continuation of Something Great,"* (Thomas Nelson Incorporated, 1995), 68.

[2] Linal Harris, *"Are you stopping 3 feet from GOLD?"* (June 2, 2013), www.inspirationalperspective.com.

Chapter 13

Attached To Our Tears

No one reading this book grew up thinking:

"I'm going to be divorced and alone by the age of 34."

"I'm going to be ostracized from my kids because of the decisions I have made."

"I'm going to be financially destitute because of my addiction."

"I'm going to get cancer at 42."

"I'm going to be fired from my job at 55."

"I'm going to watch my daughter or my son marry someone that I hate."

"I'm going to have a child in prison."

"I'm going to bury my 21 year old son or daughter."

I've been in the homes of people who have lost teenage sons or daughters. It is gripping, and it is heart breaking. Maybe you are experiencing heartbreak in this moment. Maybe God promised you something and it has yet to come to reality, and you've been waiting and waiting and waiting on God to come through. Let me tell you, these are the moments when your faith is laid bare on the altar and is hanging by a single thread. What do you do when life doesn't turn out the way you thought it should? There's a story that is found in 2 Kings chapter 20. It's a story about King Hezekiah.

"About that time Hezekiah became deathly ill, and the prophet Isaiah son of Amoz went to visit him" (2 Kings 20:1a, NLT).

Who exactly was King Hezekiah? Chapter 18 of 2 Kings really introduces us to him before this tragic moment in his life.

"Hezekiah son of Ahaz began to rule over Judah in the third year of King Hoshea's reign in Israel. ² He was twenty-five years old when he became king, and he reigned in Jerusalem twenty-nine years. His mother was Abijah, the daughter of Zechariah. ³ He did what was pleasing in the Lord's sight, just as his ancestor David had done. ⁴ He removed the pagan shrines, smashed the sacred pillars, and cut down the Asherah poles. He broke up the bronze serpent that Moses had made, because the people of Israel had been offering sacrifices to it. The bronze serpent was called Nehushtan. ⁵ Hezekiah trusted in the Lord, the God of Israel. There was no one like him among all the kings of Judah, either before or after his time. ⁶ He remained faithful to the Lord in everything, and he carefully obeyed all the commands the Lord had given Moses. ⁷ So the Lord was with him, and Hezekiah was successful in everything he did" (2 Kings 18:1-7a, NLT).

Wouldn't you like to have something like this said and written about you? *"There was no one like him among all the kings of Judah, either before or after his time,"* and *"he remained faithful to the Lord in everything."*

But, when you fast forward to chapter 20, you have him lying on his deathbed. The prophet Isaiah comes to visit, and this is what he says to him:

He gave the king this message: "This is what the Lord says: Set your affairs in order, for you are going to die. You will not recover from this illness" (2 Kings 20:1b, NLT).

No doubt this was a scary message to receive, but I want you to notice King Hezekiah's reaction to this news.

When Hezekiah heard this, he turned his face to the wall and prayed to the Lord, ³ "Remember, O Lord, how I have always been faithful to you and have served you single-mindedly, always doing what pleases you." Then he broke down and wept bitterly (2 Kings 20:2-3, NLT).

He didn't scoff. He didn't say, *"Watch me."* His heart didn't fill up with pride. He went to the only One that could heal him, and he wept bitterly in His presence. He just cried to the Lord.

Have you ever done that? I have so many times. It was as if he was crying out to God saying, *"I don't have anywhere to go but to You."* That's the place that the Lord is trying to get everyone to. *"Lord, I don't have anything without You, and I don't have anywhere to go but to You."*

Do you know something about tears? They never go unnoticed by the Lord. Psalm 56 is a Psalm of David when he was in a troubled situation.

"You keep track of all my sorrows. You have collected all my tears in your bottle. You have recorded each one in your book" (Psalm 56:8, NLT).

David says that God collects our tears in His bottle, and He records each one in His book. Do you know what you can definitively say about God when you read that verse? God has attached Himself to our tears.

In John 11, you have Jesus weeping near the grave of His friend Lazarus. Why was He weeping? Was He angry at the unbelief of the people? Probably. Was He angry at the brokenness of the world caused by sin? Yes. Was He moved in His spirit to tears because these were His friends enduring this pain? More than likely. Through the inspiration of the Holy Spirit, David writes these words:

"The Lord is close to the brokenhearted; he rescues those whose spirits

are crushed" (Psalm 34:18, NLT).

This is the heart of Jesus. This is one of the reasons why He wept. He's close to the brokenhearted and to the broken hearts that we encounter as finite, human beings. I want you to notice how the Lord responds to King Hezekiah's tears:

But before Isaiah had left the middle courtyard, this message came to him from the Lord: ⁵ "Go back to Hezekiah, the leader of my people. Tell him, 'This is what the Lord, the God of your ancestor David, says: I have heard your prayer and seen your tears. I will heal you, and three days from now you will get out of bed and go to the Temple of the Lord. ⁶ I will add fifteen years to your life, and I will rescue you and this city from the king of Assyria. I will defend this city for my own honor and for the sake of my servant David'" (2 Kings 20:4-6, NLT).

Whoa! What did the Lord say to Hezekiah? He said, *"I will heal you. Three days from now, you will get out of bed and go to the Temple of the Lord, and I will add fifteen years to your life. I will rescue you and this city from the king of Assyria."*

Why did He say this to Hezekiah? What was the reason? Did you catch it? *"I have heard your prayer and seen your tears."* Isn't that wonderful? That was all God needed to see and hear. He loves His children. He sees our tears, and He is moved by them because He has attached Himself to them.

I cannot think of a greater passage that shows that God is attached to our tears and moved by our tears, than the story that is found in Luke chapter 7 about the widow of Nain.

Soon afterward Jesus went with his disciples to the village of Nain, and a large crowd followed him. ¹² A funeral procession was coming out as he approached the village gate. The young man who had died was a widow's only son, and a large crowd from the village was with her. ¹³ When the Lord saw her, his heart overflowed with compassion. "Don't cry!" he said. ¹⁴ Then he walked over to the coffin and touched it, and the bearers stopped. "Young man," he said, "I tell you, get up."

¹⁵ *Then the dead boy sat up and began to talk! And Jesus gave him back to his mother.* ¹⁶ *Great fear swept the crowd, and they praised God, saying, "A mighty prophet has risen among us," and "God has visited his people today."* ¹⁷ *And the news about Jesus spread throughout Judea and the surrounding countryside* (Luke 7:11-17, NLT).

Let's set the scene. Jesus and His disciples are walking toward the village of Nain, which is not too far from Capernaum. Jesus has just come from that area, performing a miracle of healing the sick servant of a Roman Centurion. Remember him? *"Just say the word and my servant will be healed."*

Imagine the scene. There is this joyous celebration when the servant is healed, and you have a great crowd following Jesus walking towards the village of Nain. Notice what they are about to encounter.

"A funeral procession was coming out as he approached the village gate. The young man who had died was a widow's only son, and a large crowd from the village was with her" (Luke 7:12, NLT).

What did they encounter? An entirely different crowd. The crowd with Jesus is joyful, happy, celebrating, full of life—they were with Jesus. This funeral crowd was the exact opposite: sorrowful, mournful, hopeless, and despondent. I find it fascinating that just as Jesus is arriving into the city gate of Nain, this funeral procession is coming out. Do you think that was by accident? No!

Remember the encounter with the woman at the well? *"And He had to go through Samaria."*

This meeting of these two crowds was not by accident but by divine providence of the Living God! It is perfect timing by the perfect God.

We are not told how this young man died or how old he was or even his name. What we are told is this was the only son of an already made widow. What does this now mean for her moving forward? She has lost her husband and has now lost her only son. It means that she is truly all alone in a society that did not have provision to care for people like her.

She was now left unprotected and unprovided for. Her future was very bleak, and this was a very big deal. Her grief in this moment would have been the epitome of grief that would accompany bitter weeping. In other words, in this culture, there was no greater sorrow.

In this crowd you would have friends and loved ones accompanying her, but also you would have professional musicians and professional mourners who would wail and mourn on behalf of the deceased and those who were still living without them. This would have been a very loud, demonstrative, dramatic scene, and you have Jesus about to enter right into the midst of it. We are not told all of the details in this story, but we are told of one detail that can bring hope to every situation.

When the Lord saw her, his heart overflowed with compassion. "Don't cry!" he said (Luke 7:13, NLT).

He doesn't mourn for the young man lying dead. He mourns for her. *"When the Lord saw her."* He mourns for this woman who has already lost her husband. He mourns for this mother who has just lost her only son. It is for her that His heart overflows with compassion.

That word, *"Compassion"* literally means *"affecting the inner parts of the body."* It signifies that Jesus felt this human emotion in the depth of his heart and in the bottom of His gut. It is one of the most tender moments of Jesus in all of the Bible. He was moved into action by the real tears of this woman. *"Don't cry!"* Look at how else Jesus jumps into action.

"Then he walked over to the coffin and touched it, and the bearers stopped" (Luke 7:14a, NLT).

This is interesting. He interrupts the entire procession, and He touches the coffin, which is something that was never done, because at this point, He is now considered to be ceremonially unclean. However, Jesus didn't care about such things. He was moved to action by the tears of this woman.

Picture this tremendous scene. The funeral procession is stopped and both crowds, the mournful and the joyous, are now standing in silence wondering, *"What is He going to do?"* It's an awkward moment to say the least, and all eyes are on Jesus. The bearers had to stop when Jesus touched the coffin. His act would have been seen as offensive and adding to her grief, interrupting this solemn moment, but Jesus had already looked at her and was moved by her tears, and it is not an interruption when the King of Glory enters in! Look at what Jesus says in this moment.

"Young man," he said, "I tell you, get up" (Luke 7:14, NLT).

Luke's Gospel is the only one to give us an account of this resurrection miracle, and he makes no mention of Jesus making some elaborate scene. He simply speaks. It was good that Jesus told this specific young man to get up, for if He had just said, *"Get up"* all the dead people on earth would have walked out of their graves! Look at the power that happens when the Lord speaks.

"Then the dead boy sat up and began to talk!" (Luke 7:15a, NLT).

I'm sure at this point, everyone watching this is in complete shock. It's a good thing that the boy opened his mouth and spoke, for had he not, could you imagine? Jesus would have had to pick up every person in attendance after they fainted! I love the special thing that Jesus does next. Don't miss this.

"And Jesus gave him back to his mother" (Luke 7:15b, NLT).

It does not say that *"Jesus took a bow,"* or that Jesus said to the crowd, *"Now do you believe Me?"* No, the text simply says, that Jesus gave this young man back to his mother. You need to understand that this miracle was not done for the benefit for anyone else. Jesus hurt for this hurting widowed mom, and He healed her hurt because He is moved by our tears.

This is the entire purpose of this passage! It is to show that God is attached to and moved by our tears. He was moved by the tears of King Hezekiah, and He was moved by the tears of this woman, and He is moved by your tears.

He sees them, and He collects them in His bottle, and records them in His book. Let me ask you. Do you need to cry out to God about anything? Do you need to weep in the Lord's presence over anything? He is close to the brokenhearted, and He is moved by our tears. Cry out to the Lord in your heartache, confusion, suffering, and grief. The Lord is attached to our tears.

Chapter 14

Attached To Surrender

I will never forget a conversation I had on an airplane flying from the U.S. to Africa. Seated next to me was a woman who had her master's degree in Theology from seminary, who now no longer believes in the existence of God. Logically, I start saying things to her like, *"What about this?"* or *"What about that?"* I felt confident I could convince her back to belief using the natural realm, but she was not budging.

Finally, at some point the conversation, the Holy Spirit prompted me to say these words to her: *"What happened in your life that made you walk away from God?"*

Tears started to well up in her eyes, and here's what she said. *"I asked God for something, and He didn't come through. I concluded that He must no longer exist."*

She gave no further details, but she had opened her heart. Before I could pry any deeper, she said these words, *"And don't talk to me about surrender."*

When we don't agree with the one who calls the shots, our reaction is often the same. *"Maybe, God, You are not the right one for the job."*

I'm sure we've all been there at some point in our Christian lives, feeling the same way when God's ways don't seem to make sense. I often think about John the Baptist, sitting in a prison cell, saying these words: *"Are you the Christ, or should we be looking for someone else?"*

Did he really say that? *"No, no, no God. You don't do it this way. Obedient living results in health and wealth and safety and everything working out right, right?"*

It is in those moments of despair that we trust God, that we surrender to His plan and lay ours down, or we don't. It's a point of entry that God requires everyone to succumb to. There is no salvation without surrender. There is no God encounter without surrender to Him first, and even in your Christian walk with the Lord, He continues to ask you to surrender to His ways and His Lordship.

He asks for surrender because He's attached to it, and because He is attached to it, He will not move in your life until you walk through the door of surrender. Just ask Abraham. Remember him? His story is found in Genesis chapter 12.

The Lord had said to Abram, "Leave your native country, your relatives, and your father's family, and go to the land that I will show you. ² I will make you into a great nation. I will bless you and make you famous, and you will be a blessing to others. ³ I will bless those who bless you and curse those who treat you with contempt. All the families on earth will be blessed through you." ⁴ So Abram departed as the Lord had instructed, and Lot went with him. Abram was seventy-five years old when he left Haran (Genesis 12:1-4, NLT).

He is 75 years old when God calls out to him. He is 100 years old when this promise is finally realized.

"The Lord kept his word and did for Sarah exactly what he had promised. ² She became pregnant, and she gave birth to a son for Abraham in his old age. This happened at just the time God had said it would. ³ And Abraham named their son Isaac" (Genesis 21:1-3, NLT).

For 25 years, Abraham and Sarah wait for the promise of God to come to fruition. That's a long time of waiting, but the promise is finally realized, and they are overjoyed. For about 15 years or so, everything is great. Abraham is watching his promised son grow up. Abraham is envisioning the future for his son and waiting for him to get married. Things are good, and Abraham is finally at peace with God. He's no longer waiting, and he's received the promise of God, and he gets to hug his promised son every night. Isn't God great? Then we get to one of the most tension-filled passages in all of the Bible—Genesis 22.

Some time later, God tested Abraham's faith. "Abraham!" God called.

"Yes," he replied. "Here I am" (Genesis 22:1, NLT).

Notice the word *"tested."* Right off the bat we know that God is up to something. The severity of the request you are about to read has to be seen through this lens—this is a test from Almighty God.

"Take your son, your only son—yes, Isaac, whom you love so much— and go to the land of Moriah. Go and sacrifice him as a burnt offering on one of the mountains, which I will show you" (Genesis 22:2, NLT).

Let me briefly explain child sacrifice. God did not condone child sacrifice. The Old Testament explicitly forbids it, and God judged nations and brought disaster on nations who practiced it.

He calls those children sacrificed *"My children,"* because God loves children.

So why does He call Abraham to do this? He's testing his faith. Is Abraham willing to offer God that which is most precious to him? You say, *"But, Pastor Matt, this was God's promise to Abraham. This is the fulfillment of God's dream in his life. Why would God ask him for this?"* It's what God asks every one of us as well, because He is attached to surrender.

What do you do with the promise when it finally turns into a reality? When you finally get married, when you finally have children, when you finally get the dream job that you've been praying for, when you finally start dating the girl you've always dreamed about dating, when your career finally takes off, when you finally get your dream home? Let's rephrase God's request to Abraham:

"Take your dream, your only dream—yes, that dream, that you love so much…go and sacrifice that dream as a burnt offering to Me."

What do you do when the promise is finally realized? You give the dream back to God. Understand this about God: He's attached to surrender, and when God gives you your dream, He is going to ask for it back. He's going to ask you to surrender that dream to Him. He's going to ask you to entrust that dream over to His care. He's going to ask you to allow Him to determine the outcome of the dream. Why? It's His dream for you. It's not your dream.

There is never a moment in our lives where we have permission to be unsurrendered to God in any area. Read that again. Underline it. Make sure you grasp it. God requires surrender, because He's attached to it. When a dream remains unsurrendered to God, something happens:

The dream that is realized often turns into the idol that we worship.

The God-given dream often replaces God. Most of the time, the consequences are unintended. Think about moms and children for one second. Mom's love their children. The problem becomes when they hold them so tightly that they unintentionally squeeze God out of it. *"I will protect him"* or *"I'm not letting her out of my sight."* Do you know any parents like that?

Think about marriages for one second. *"I got him, it's my job to keep him." "I'm going to control her so that she does what I want."*

Think about finances. *"I make this money; I can do what I want to with it."*

Think about the dream job. *"I got myself here. It's my job to keep myself here."*

And we squeeze and we squeeze and we own it and possess it until we finally get to the point where we begin to worship it. It's something that God never intended. God wanted Abraham to worship the God of the dream, not the dream itself, so He asked for it back. Here's what I can promise you. I promise you that He will eventually ask for your dream back as well.

Phil Vischer, the founder of *Veggie Tales*, eventually lost everything he had worked so hard for.

His dream was taken away, and here's what he said about it:

"If God gives you a dream, and the dream comes to life and God shows up in it, and then the dream dies, it may be that God wants to see what is more important to you—the dream or Him." [1]

The dream when not given back ultimately becomes your god. This is why the dream must have an ALTAR-CATION. It must be laid on the altar. Here's what Watchman Nee says:

"We approach God like little children with open hands, begging for gifts. Because God is a good God, he fills our hands with good things like life, health, friends, wealth, success, good kids, a good home, a good marriage. We rejoice in what we have received and run around comparing what we have with what others have. But at some point, when our hands are finally full, God says, "My child, I long to have fellowship with you. Reach out your hand and take my hand." But, we can't because our hands are full. God says, "Put those things aside and take my hand." We cry, "No, we can't. It's too hard to put them down." God says, "But I am the one who gave them to you in the first place." "O God, what you have asked for is too hard. Please don't ask us to put those things aside." And God answers quietly, "You must." [2]

When my children were little and still sleeping in a crib, I would do something with them virtually every night. I would lift them up over the crib and place them down in it, and by doing that natural motion, I mimicked the same motion as an offering. Every night that I put them to bed, I made my children an offering to God. I had an ALTAR—CAT-

ION. *"Lord, they are Yours not mine."*

In my previous study at my former church, there was a chair. In that chair, I spent time with God. One morning in my study, I had an AL-TAR—CATION. I emptied everything out of my pockets and began laying them down in the seat of the chair as I was on my knees.

My keys which represented the home and the vehicles that I owned,

My wallet which represented the credit cards and everything I financially possessed,

The pictures of my children—*"Lord, you can have my children,"*

A picture of my wife—*"Lord, you can have my marriage,"*

My watch representing my time, my schedule,

My Bible—representing my ministry.

I put in that chair everything I could think of. As tears rolled down my face, I laid myself on the altar of God in that moment. God will lead you to an ALTAR—CATION because He is attached to surrender. He will ask you to lay that dream on His altar. In a recent article about Chip and Joanna Gaines, Joanna said this about their business:

One key time Joanna Gaines heard the voice of God was during her second pregnancy. She and her husband Chip decided to close their store, Magnolia Market, so she could focus on raising their children. Opening the business had been a dream come true, so closing its doors was difficult and emotional for Joanna.

"I remember the last day, you know, we're closing the shop down, and I'm crying because I feel like it's the end of a dream," Gaines said. "I hear God say, very clearly, he said, 'Joanna, if you trust me with your dreams, I'm going to take Magnolia further than you could've ever dreamed, so just trust me.'" She said that she immediately felt at peace after hearing those words. [3]

Will it be tough to surrender? Yes. Do you think it was tough for Abraham or Joanna Gaines? Yes. But, do you think it will be worth it? Absolutely! When God asks, you have to understand that He is on the other side of that point of surrender, waiting for you!

Jesus is there, with all of His power and all of His resources! Because God is attached to surrender, it also means that there are other things waiting for you when you surrender. It is exactly what Abraham experienced as a result of giving up his dream, Isaac.

Genuine Peace

In this account of Abraham, you never see Abraham in conflict. He's not ringing his hands and pacing back and forth. Notice what it says in Genesis 22.

"The next morning Abraham got up early. He saddled his donkey and took two of his servants with him, along with his son, Isaac. Then he chopped wood for a fire for a burnt offering and set out for the place God had told him about" (Genesis 22:3, NLT).

He walks up the mountain, he takes the knife, and he's ready to do whatever God wants. He is completely surrendered to God in this moment. How do I know he's in peace? Look at what the book of Hebrews has to say about him.

"Abraham reasoned that if Isaac died, God was able to bring him back to life again. And in a sense, Abraham did receive his son back from the dead" (Hebrews 11:19, NLT).

He was so assured in the promise of God that even if God somehow let this plan go through, God was going to raise Isaac back up from the dead. This is what Abraham genuinely believed, and that's what the altar brings, genuine peace. It is the kind of peace where you don't have to worry anymore or try to control and manipulate the circumstances because you know that God has it all taken care of. Pastor and author Chuck Swindoll tells an amazing story to illustrate this.

There was a man who gave his business to God. He had hassled over it for years. He had wrestled with it and fought it for two decades.

One day he decided, "I've had it; that's enough!" He had heard from his pastor that Sunday morning about the value of turning his entire business over to God. It was when he drove away from church that he decided he has worried enough. By the time he got home, he had totally and unequivocally committed his business to God.

That very night his place of business caught on fire. He got an emergency call. He rather calmly drove down to the commercial residence and was standing on the street, watching the place go up in flames. He was sort of smiling to himself. One of his colleagues raced to his side and questioned his relaxed attitude about what was happening. "Man! Don't you know what's happening to you?...It's...it's burning up!"

He replied, "I know it. I know it. No problem, Fred. This morning I gave this company to God, and if He wants to burn it up, that's His business."[4]

Surrender also brings about something else.

True Worship

On the third day of their journey, Abraham looked up and saw the place in the distance.[5] "Stay here with the donkey," Abraham told the servants. "The boy and I will travel a little farther. We will worship there, and then we will come right back" (Genesis 22:4-5, NLT).

Abraham viewed this ALTAR-CATION as time of worship. *"We will worship, and then we will come back."* Can I tell you something? The altar always leads to worship. Look at how the Apostle Paul describes the sacrificial life.

"Therefore, I urge you, brothers and sisters, in view of God's mercy, to offer your bodies as a living sacrifice, holy and pleasing to God—this is your true and proper worship" (Romans 12:1, NIV).

What is the sacrifice that is holy and pleasing to God? It is when our bodies, our whole selves, are placed on the altar of surrender. This is the worship that God wants because He's attached to surrender, and His power is made know through those who are fully surrendered to Him. Surrender leads to true and proper worship, and whether it's your dream or yourself, the altar is where true worship takes place. You can't worship God without going to the altar of surrender.

Divine Encounter

When they arrived at the place where God had told him to go, Abraham built an altar and arranged the wood on it. Then he tied his son, Isaac, and laid him on the altar on top of the wood. ^{10} And Abraham picked up the knife to kill his son as a sacrifice. ^{11} At that moment the angel of the Lord called to him from heaven, "Abraham! Abraham!"

"Yes," Abraham replied. "Here I am!" ^{12} "Don't lay a hand on the boy!" the angel said. "Do not hurt him in any way, for now I know that you truly fear God. You have not withheld from me even your son, your only son" (Genesis 22:9-12, NLT).

In his moment of surrendering everything to God, fulling trusting the Lord and His plan, God showed up. He experienced the manifest presence of God. If you want to experience the presence of God in your life, meet the Lord often in the place of surrender because that's where He is, that's what He's attached to, and that's where He makes Himself known.

Supernatural Provision

Then Abraham looked up and saw a ram caught by its horns in a thicket. So he took the ram and sacrificed it as a burnt offering in place of his son. ^{14} Abraham named the place Yahweh-Yireh (which means "the Lord will provide"). To this day, people still use that name as a proverb: "On the mountain of the Lord it will be provided" (Genesis 22:13-14, NLT).

Abraham named that place of surrender, *"the Lord will provide,"* and he saw the Lord provide for him in a miraculous way. That's what happens when you meet the Lord in the place of surrender. He does things that can only be accomplished in His power, not our own.

Full Blessing

Then the angel of the Lord called again to Abraham from heaven.

[16] "This is what the Lord says: Because you have obeyed me and have not withheld even your son, your only son, I swear by my own name that [17] I will certainly bless you. I will multiply your descendants beyond number, like the stars in the sky and the sand on the seashore. Your descendants will conquer the cities of their enemies. [18] And through your descendants all the nations of the earth will be blessed—all because you have obeyed me" (Genesis 22:15-18, NLT).

"Because you've laid your dream on the altar, Abraham, I'm going to take that dream and show you the full extent of it." As I've made it clear before in this book, obedience always brings God's blessings, and when you look closely at the magnitude of this blessing from the Lord, it wasn't just given to Abraham but to all the nations of the earth! It was the fullest extent of God's blessing on his life. Don't you want that kind of blessing from the Lord as well? I love how the story ends.

"Then they returned to the servants and traveled back to Beersheba, where Abraham continued to live" (Genesis 22:19, NLT).

Isn't that great? He just lived! Understand, you will never truly live in peace, in true worship, in the presence of God with His divine provision and supernatural blessing, until you succumb to the altar of surrender. Until you truly trust your dream and yourself into God's total care, you will never understand that it is the designed place and the best possible place to live.

Whatever He's asking for, give it to Him. Let Him, the good God, who knows what is best for you because He created you, let Him take control of it. Live in the land of surrender, and begin to truly live just like Abraham did.

---

[1] Phil Vischer, "Me, Myself, and Bob: A True Story About Dreams, God, and Talking Vegetables," (Thomas Nelson Inc, 2008), 235.

[2] Ray Pritchard, "What Is Your Isaac?" (August 27, 2008), www.keep-believing.com.

[3] Lauren Richards, "Joanna Gaines Once Told Oprah Her Relationship With Religion Was 'Like No One Else's'," (The List, July 16, 2023), www.thelist.com.

[4] Charles R. Swindoll, "Swindoll's Ultimate Book of Illustrations & Quotes," (Thomas Nelson, Nashville, 1998), 239-240.

Chapter 15

Attached To Humility

Jesus always had the right response at the right time. He was never taken off guard or at a loss for words. He knew exactly what to say, and He meant exactly every word that came out of His mouth. There is this awesome story found in Luke 18 that demonstrates Jesus' favorite subject, the Kingdom of God, and it came at a moment when the disciples clearly couldn't see it.

One day some parents brought their little children to Jesus so he could touch and bless them. But when the disciples saw this, they scolded the parents for bothering him. ¹⁶ Then Jesus called for the children and said to the disciples, "Let the children come to me. Don't stop them! For the Kingdom of God belongs to those who are like these children. ¹⁷ I tell you the truth, anyone who doesn't receive the Kingdom of God like a child will never enter it" (Luke 18:15-17, NLT).

Let's set the scene. Jesus and his disciples are hanging out and some parents bring their children to Jesus so that He could touch them and bless them. *"Little children"* in Luke's account refers to *"infants."* Other Gospels use a word to describe *"little children."* What you have here are parents with small children ranging more than likely from infancy to those just beginning to walk, bringing them to Jesus. Some have taken the phrase *"touch and bless"* as alluding to infant baptism, but this is not the case at all. These parents wanted their children to be near to Jesus and touched by Jesus, God in the flesh. Who wouldn't want that for their child? I guess the disciples.

The text says that when these parents began to gather around Jesus, the disciples took notice and scolded these parents for *"bothering"* Jesus. They thought that this is what Jesus wanted. Why? The obvious reason is that Jesus had *"way more important people"* to see, and *"way more important people"* to attend. In their mind, Jesus did not have time to be *"bothered"* by these *"little people."* What benefit could they possibly provide for Jesus' ministry and advancement? Did you notice Jesus' reaction?

Then Jesus called for the children and said to the disciples, "Let the children come to me. Don't stop them! For the Kingdom of God belongs to those who are like these children" (Luke 18:16, NLT).

Aren't you thankful that Jesus is not bothered by such things as corporate or ministry advancement and outward façade'? He never has been. He cares only about what many of us overlook: *"The least of these."*

The King will reply, "Truly I tell you, whatever you did for one of the least of these brothers and sisters of mine, you did for me" (Matthew 25:40, NLT).

The least of these. This includes such people as those in prison, those who are hungry, those who are in need of clothing and shelter. He says that whatever you did for them, you have done for Me.

"If a man has a hundred sheep and one of them gets lost, what will he do? Won't he leave the ninety-nine others in the wilderness and go to search for the one that is lost until he finds it?" (Luke 15:4, NLT).

Isn't this exactly what God does for us? He leaves the 99 in search of the one who is lost. It's very interesting to read Mark's interpretation of this event concerning Jesus and the little children. He describes it in a little bit more detail.

*"When Jesus saw what was happening, he was **angry** with his disciples"* (Mark 10:14a, NLT, emphasis mine).

Mark, dictated to by Peter, describes Jesus as being *"angry"* with his disciples for preventing these parents and children from coming to Him. It begs the question, *"Why?"* Why is Jesus so angry? Why does He say, *"Don't stop them?"*

"For the Kingdom of God belongs to those who are like these children" (Luke 18:16b, NLT).

The disciples missed the very thing that Jesus was about, and Jesus lets them know it. Make no mistake that Jesus was placing a huge emphasis on the priority of children, however, He was making an even bigger point about the Kingdom of God. This is Jesus' priority. Let's define it.

The Kingdom of God is mentioned over 120 times in the messages of Jesus in the Gospels. Jesus talked about it all the time. It refers to one thing:

The rule and reign of God on this earth, to which every person who has ever been created has to submit.

This is what Jesus has come to announce, and He has given His followers the task of announcing the terms of His gracious, perfect rule to every person they encounter. It is the rule and authority of God that comes to subdue our sinful hearts.

Jesus tells the disciples and everyone listening in on the conversation that the Kingdom of God, belongs to those who are just like these children. Physically? No. In a spiritual sense? Yes. Think about it. What do you know about little children? Let me give you some obvious truths.

Totally Dependent

A baby cannot do anything on its own. If left to itself, it will die. It is totally helpless and totally dependent on someone else to take care of it especially for the necessary task of simple survival.

Extravagantly Needy

They need us for everything. They need us to provide food for them, to buckle them into their car seats, to make sure there are no dangerous objects or chokeable things lying around them. As they get older, they need us for advice, and direction and encouragement. According to research, how many years does it take until a child develops a fully mature brain and makes the transition into adulthood? Twenty-five years.[1] During that whole time, they are extravagantly needy.

Innocently Trusting

Children will believe that you are good and that what you tell them is the truth, until you prove to be untrustworthy. Isn't that right? A few years ago, one of my children walked into my office where I had a cut out picture of me in a superman costume sitting on my bookshelf. Someone had given it to me. When my 5-year old saw it, he said, *"Dad, you didn't tell me you were a superhero! Why didn't you tell me you were a superhero?" "What super hero powers do you have?"* He really believed I was a super hero! By the way, I have since done nothing to persuade him of anything contrary to this notion even now that he is much older! It just proves my point that children are innocently trusting.

Fully Loving

Children come into this world giving you all the love that they have, and they long to give love and feel love. There are major emotional implications when love is not given and received this way. The critical ages for brain development and emotional well-being are in the formative years of 0-5. Experts believe that those years, the early years, are some of the most crucial years of our lives.

In many orphanages around the world, they are so overcrowded with babies that they cannot be attended to except for feeding, changing, or being bathed—survival things only. They are not held, sung to, read to, or tucked into bed. If you talk to people who have been in these environments, they all say the same things. It's eerily silent. When cries are not answered they no longer cry.

Brutally Honest

Kids tell you exactly how they feel, and they tell you exactly what they think about someone. They blurt things out about people's behavior or looks or smell or clothing. Isn't that right? There have been several television shows built around the brutal honesty of little children. Have you encountered a brutally honest child? They are not trying to be mean. They are just being honest. Think about all of these things that I mentioned:

Totally Dependent,

Extravagantly Needy,

Innocently Trusting,

Fully Loving,

Brutally Honest.

Jesus says that the kingdom of Heaven belongs to such as these. As a matter of fact, look at what He further says in the next verse.

*"I tell you the truth, anyone who doesn't receive the Kingdom of God like a child **will never enter it"*** (Luke 18:17, NLT, emphasis mine).

Not only does the Kingdom of God belong to such as these little children, Jesus says that no one will ever enter the Kingdom of God without becoming like a little child! What does it require of any adult to become like a child in Jesus' eyes? One word: Humility. You can say it like this in reference to God.

God is Attached to Humility

Think about it. To paraphrase, this is, in essence, what Jesus is saying. *"Unless you humble yourself and spiritually become like a little child, you can never enter the Kingdom of Heaven."* How do you that? Through humility. Think back to everything I previously mentioned about a little child. Those same characteristics, spiritually speaking, should be characteristic of anyone wanting entrance into the Kingdom of God.

Totally Dependent

Just like an infant is totally dependent and totally helpless on its own, so too is every person that comes to God. Entrance into the Kingdom of God is predicated on the fact that there's nothing you can do on your own to get to God. There's no amount of good works that can satisfy God or pay Him off.

"But when the kindness and love of God our Savior appeared, ⁵ he saved us, not because of righteous things we had done, but because of his mercy. He saved us through the washing of rebirth and renewal by the Holy Spirit, ⁶ whom he poured out on us generously through Jesus Christ our Savior, ⁷ so that, having been justified by his grace, we might become heirs having the hope of eternal life" (Titus 3:4-7, NIV).

Totally dependent is you getting to the place spiritually when you realize that Jesus' death on the cross is the only thing that can save you.

Extravagantly Needy

It is realizing your need for God. You need Him to save you, to forgive your sin, to cleanse you and make you right with Him. You need Him for living, breathing, and functioning in every single way. When Paul was in the city of Athens, he preached a powerful sermon on top of Mars Hill. He told the intellectual elite about their need for God.

"He is the God who made the world and everything in it. Since he is Lord of heaven and earth, he doesn't live in man-made temples, ²⁵ and human hands can't serve his needs—for he has no needs. He himself gives life and breath to everything, and he satisfies every need" (Acts 17: 24-25, NLT).

He has no needs, yet He satisfies every need. Paul goes on to preach that He now commands everyone in the world to repent and recognize His authority. You and I need the Lord, and we were never designed to live apart from Him. It takes humility to recognize this, which can only be given by God.

Innocently Trusting

What God says in His Word, you understand and believe as Truth. This is not blind faith. This is done by the work of the Holy Spirit who lives in every true child of God.

"The person without the Spirit does not accept the things that come from the Spirit of God but considers them foolishness, and cannot understand them because they are discerned only through the Spirit" (1 Corinthians 2:14, NIV).

Anyone living without the Holy Spirit cannot discern spiritual things. This means that what the Holy Spirit has written in the Scriptures has been veiled to their understanding. It is only through the Holy Spirit that we can understand the Word of God, and those who have been activated by Him, know that what they read and believe is the Truth.

Fully Loving

"This is love: not that we loved God, but that he loved us and sent his Son as an atoning sacrifice for our sins" (1 John 4:10, NIV).

The Kingdom of God belongs to those who have received and walk in the love of God. Once we used to be God haters. Now we have been turned into God lovers! This is His doing, not ours. He started it. He set His affection on us, and He placed the Holy Spirit in us to return that love to Him. This is the purpose of life, and it is an amazing gift when it is revealed by our loving Lord.

Brutally Honest

Humility, true humility, doesn't pretend. It doesn't well up with pride when coming before God. It doesn't boast. It only confesses the true condition of who we are. When Jesus hopped into Simon Peter's boat and performed the miraculous catch of fish, Peter ultimately recognized that it was the God of the universe sitting in his vessel, and he saw the true condition of his heart.

When Simon Peter saw this, he fell at Jesus' knees and said, "Go away from me, Lord; I am a sinful man!" (Luke 5:8, NIV).

You can't help but be honest when you truly come before God, not pretending but expressing to Him who you really are—sinful, broken, dirty, and powerless to change. It confesses loudly and often, *"Lord, I need You."* This is where the Kingdom of God is.

All of these require humility. God is attached to it, and you can't come to God without it. Pride, the very opposite of humility is abhorrent to God. He's repulsed by it and opposes it.

"God opposes the proud but gives grace to the humble" (James 4:6b, NLT).

Do you know that God actually stands in the way of the proud? He resists everything they try to do. He stands on the opposite side and actually fights against them. But to the humble, He gives grace! Grace! He's attached to humility, and you can always come to Him through that door. It's living a life before Him that says,

"Lord, I'm depending upon You for everything."

"Lord, I'm needy for You, Your presence and Your Word."

"Lord, I'm trusting you for my every need."

"Lord, I know that You are good, and that You are Love. I choose to love You above all else."

"Lord, if I'm being honest today, I'm anxious, I'm discouraged, I'm hurting. Be near me today."

Jesus says that this is how you get into the Kingdom, and this is how you live in the Kingdom, with humility. He says that you will never enter the Kingdom of God until you come to God like this, like a child.

The door into the Kingdom, into where God is and Heaven is, is small and narrow. It is big enough only for a little child's heart to enter. It forces you to get on your knees before God in humility. It forces you to come empty handed into His presence, not with loads of good deeds but with a simple, childlike faith. If you have never come to God like a little child, come to Him today in humility. He's attached to it.

---

[1] Stephen Johnson, *"Why is 18 the age of adulthood if the brain can take 30 years to mature?"* (Neuropsych, January 31, 2022), www.bigthink.com.

Chapter 16

Attached To Holiness

Have you ever heard of the Puritan pastor named Thomas Brooks? I had not either until I came across some of his writings. In the year 1662, he began to preach on a passage of Scripture, one verse, actually. He preached on that one verse for 58 straight sermons! When he began preaching, this is what he told his congregation about this verse:

"So I say, had I Chrysostom's tongue, head, and heart, and were I every way advantaged to preach a sermon to the whole world, I would choose to preach on this text before any other in the Bible." [1]

Wow! That's a big statement. One chance to preach to one world audience on one passage of Scripture before any other in the Bible. What do you think it could be? Here it is.

"Make every effort to live in peace with everyone and to be holy; without holiness no one will see the Lord" (Hebrews 12:14, NLT).

Did you catch what the verse said? *"Without holiness no one will see the Lord."* Clearly, by this one verse, we know that God is attached to holiness. Without holiness, no one has a hope of seeing the Lord, but what does it mean? Let me first address what it doesn't mean, and then we can formulate what God is actually saying in the text.

The first part of the verse says, *"Make every effort..."* When people pair that with *"holiness,"* they automatically assume that it is referring to our righteousness, our effort, our holiness. They naturally say something like this when they hear this verse, *"That's my job. He must be talking about my efforts. He must be talking about my righteousness,"* and they couldn't be more wrong. What does the Bible say about our *"righteousness?"*

"We are all infected and impure with sin. When we display our righteous deeds, they are nothing but filthy rags. Like autumn leaves, we wither and fall, and our sins sweep us away like the wind" (Isaiah 64:6, NLT).

What shall we conclude then? Do we have any advantage? Not at all! For we have already made the charge that Jews and Gentiles alike are all under the power of sin. ¹⁰As it is written: "There is no one righteous, not even one" (Romans 3:9-10a, NIV).

No one righteous. Not even one. All are infected with sin.

"Once you were dead because of your disobedience and your many sins. ²You used to live in sin, just like the rest of the world, obeying the devil—the commander of the powers in the unseen world. He is the spirit at work in the hearts of those who refuse to obey God. ³All of us used to live that way, following the passionate desires and inclinations of our sinful nature. By our very nature we were subject to God's anger, just like everyone else" (Ephesians 2:1-3, NLT).

"Once we, too, were foolish and disobedient. We were misled and became slaves to many lusts and pleasures. Our lives were full of evil and envy, and we hated each other. ⁴But—When God our Savior revealed his kindness and love, ⁵he saved us, not because of the righteous things we had done, but because of his mercy. He washed away our sins, giving us a new birth and new life through the Holy Spirit" (Titus 3:3-5 (NLT).

Did He save us because of our righteousness? No! He saved us as an act of mercy.

"For the person who keeps all of the laws except one is as guilty as a person who has broken all of God's laws" (James 2:10, NLT).

Has there ever been anyone, besides Jesus, who perfectly kept all of God's laws? No, and James sums it up by saying, *"If you've broken one, it's just as if you've broken them all."* Notice what Paul tells the Galatian believers.

"I do not treat the grace of God as meaningless. For if keeping the law could make us right with God, then there was no need for Christ to die" (Galatians 2:21, NLT).

Do you get it? How could we, who are wretched sinners, stained with sin, thoroughly guilty over and over again, how could we do anything on our own to gain righteous standing with God? No one measures up, no one meets God's standard of perfect righteousness. This is the whole reason for Jesus coming to earth; to save humanity! The Gospel means *"Good News"* because the only other news that we have is bad! We are all deserving of God's wrath. All! And yet, I'm so amazed, even with all of the evidence in Scripture, that so many people are still deceived into thinking that their good works will get them into the Kingdom of God, apart from Christ.

People who say, *"Well it is what Jesus did on the cross and what I am doing now,"* like it's *"Christ plus baptism"* or *"Christ plus circumcision"* or *"Christ plus communion."* Many theologies and religions are based off of a works-based mentality. *"I must do something to inherit salvation,"* yet this is the very opposite of what the Word of God teaches. It is not our righteousness because we have none on our own, apart from Christ! What then does *"holiness"* mean in this verse if it's not referring to our good works? Look at it again.

"Make every effort to live in peace with everyone and to be holy; without holiness no one will see the Lord" (Hebrews 12:14, NLT).

If it's not holiness on our own, then what does the passage mean? I want us to understand what the meaning of the text is, using a two point approach. The first point opens the door half-way. The second point opens the door to a full and complete understanding. Here is what the passage means.

We are made holy

We are made holy, by Jesus. The message of the Gospel is that God takes all of our sin, and charges it to Jesus' account. The Innocent died for the guilty. The Pure taking the place of the impure. In that same spiritual transaction, not only is all of our sin put upon Jesus, all of the righteousness of Jesus that He perfectly lived while on this earth is charged to our account. Because of Jesus, God now sees us as perfectly righteous, completely holy.

"God made him who had no sin to be sin for us, so that in him we might become the righteousness of God" (2 Corinthians 5:21, NIV).

This is how we are made holy. Jesus imputes His righteousness on to us and charges it to our account.

"The high priest carries the blood of animals into the Most Holy Place as a sin offering, but the bodies are burned outside the camp. ¹²And so Jesus also suffered outside the city gate to make the people holy through his own blood" (Hebrews 13:11-12, NLT).

Hebrews 13 says that we were made holy by the blood of Jesus spilled on the cross. Holiness is given to us when we come into relationship with Jesus. But, but, but, the text in Hebrews 12 plainly says, *"make every effort...to be holy."* Clearly this is not just talking just about our inherited spiritual position before God. It is that, but there is another understanding of holiness intended here.

We live holy

We are made holy by Jesus, and we now live holy. What happens when a person comes to God? That person is indwelled by the Lord Jesus, through the person of the Holy Spirit. The Holy Spirit comes to live on the inside every Christ-follower's physical body. It's like a microchip that is inserted in your body that totally reprograms you. He changes the way you think, the way you desire, the way you live, and the way you speak. Everything is now under the control of that microchip. This is what the Holy Spirit does. He changes us, giving us the new desire and longing to follow completely after God. Let me show you this understanding in Scripture.

"Therefore, my dear friends, as you have always obeyed—not only in my presence, but now much more in my absence—continue to work out your salvation with fear and trembling, ¹³ for it is God who works in you to will and to act in order to fulfill his good purpose" (Philippians 2:12-13, NLT).

Who now gives you the desire and will to live for God? God! Who now does the work and acts in you? God! Look at 2 Peter chapter 1.

"By his divine power, God has given us everything we need for living a godly life. We have received all of this by coming to know him, the one who called us to himself by means of his marvelous glory and excellence" (2 Peter 1:3, NLT).

God gives us everything we need to live a godly life. Because the Holy Spirit now dwells inside of us, what does that now make us? Holy! I've mentioned this before in my previous book, *Reverse The Arrows: Sending the Church Back to the New Testament:*

"There is no place on this earth more sacred or holy than that where a Christ-follower dwells in that moment."

Do you understand that? Because the Holy One lives in our physical body, we are now living in a holy manner. The Apostle Paul talks about this in the context of being still married to an unbeliever after a person has trusted in the mercy of Jesus. Notice how he explains this in 1 Corinthians 7.

"For the believing wife brings holiness to her marriage, and the believing husband brings holiness to his marriage" (1 Corinthians 7:14a, NLT).

The believer brings holiness into the marriage because the Holy Spirit has now entered into that person. This is how the marriage is made holy. Now, let me ask you, can we disobey God? Can God prompt us to do something and we tell Him, *"No?"* Absolutely, and God disciplines us for it, but it is our job to respond to that prompting and that working of the Holy Spirit. This is our relationship to the Holy Spirit, and this is how we truly know that God has come to live on the inside of us.

"Make every effort to be holy" means our response to the Holy Spirit. Our yielding, to allow Him to move and have His way in our lives, filling His people with the mind and the actions of Jesus. This is how you know that your life has been invaded with the holiness of God. I love this quote by Charles Spurgeon.

"You can no more make yourself holy than you could create a world. But you are wrong to despair, for Christ can do it; he can do it for you, and he can do it now. Believe on him, and that believing will be the proof that he is working in you. Trust him, and he that has suffered for thy sins, the Lion of the tribe of Judah, shall come in, and put to rout the lion of the pit. He will bruise Satan under thy feet shortly. There is no corruption too strong for him to overcome, there is no habit too firm for him to break. He can turn a lion to a lamb, and a raven to a dove. Trust him to save thee, and he will do it, whosoever thou mayest be, and whatsoever thy past life may have been." [2]

"Christ can do it" as He lives inside of our lives. The Holy Spirit will give us a hunger for the Word of God. He will give us a hunger to obey Him. He will give us a desire for Biblical community, and if those desires are not there and if you have no evidence of holiness coming to live on the inside of you, then you have not been made holy. Without that and without Him, the Holy Spirit, you will not see the Lord, because God is attached to holiness.

We are made holy when we come to Christ, imputed with the righteousness of Jesus. We are now holy vessels because the Holy Spirit has taken up residence in our lives, and we live holy lives because it is now God giving us everything we need to do so.

It is not about us or our efforts. It is all about yielding to the Holy Spirit as He works in us everything that is pleasing to the Lord. *"Without holiness no one will see the Lord"* because God is attached to holiness.

---

[1] Thomas Brooks, ed. by the Reverend Alexander Balloch Grosart, *"The Complete Works of Thomas Brooks, Vol. 4, Containing The Crown and Glory of Christianity,"* (James Nichol, Edinburgh, 1867), 35.

[2] Charles Spurgeon, *"Holiness, Without Which No Man Shall See the Lord,"* (A Sermon Delivered by C. H. Spurgeon, At the Metropolitan Tabernacle, Newington. On a Lord's-day Evening, in 1862), www. blueletterbible.org.

Chapter 17

Attached To Forgiveness

The Word of God is just that, God's Word. If you are refraining from opening it, like it was stated in an earlier chapter, you are keeping God from speaking into your life. Remember? God is attached to it. You may say things like this, *"I don't see God in my life, or I don't hear His voice."* My first question to you is always going to be, *"Are you spending any time in the Word of God?"* You cannot grow, you cannot connect with God, and you cannot enjoy the fullness of who He is, without taking time to enjoy Him in His Word.

This was true of me a few months ago. I was reading in Mark chapter 11 about Jesus cursing the fig tree. Remember that story? Jesus and His disciples were walking along, and Jesus went to pick figs off of a fig tree but none were there. Subsequently, Jesus cursed the tree. When the disciples walked by the next day, they noticed that the tree had withered and died, and then Jesus said it:

Then Jesus said to the disciples, "Have faith in God. ²³ I tell you the truth, you can say to this mountain, 'May you be lifted up and thrown into the sea,' and it will happen. But you must really believe it will happen and have no doubt in your heart. ²⁴ I tell you, you can pray for anything, and if you believe that you've received it, it will be yours" (Mark 11:22-24, NLT).

In this seemingly strange event where you have Jesus cursing a fig tree because it was barren, you have Jesus launching into a discourse about spiritual authority. Jesus says to His disciples, *"You can say to this mountain...and it will happen."* Here He doesn't say, *"Ask."* He says, *"Say."* That's spiritual authority. When I read this passage in my time with the Lord, I said, *"Jesus, I want this kind of authority."*

Jesus tells the disciples in the following verse, *"You can pray for anything, and it will be yours."* He doesn't qualify the prayer. He doesn't say to them, *"You can pray for anything as long as it's spiritual."* He doesn't say that. He says, *"Anything."*

At this point in my time with God, I became passionate with the Lord. *"Lord, what does this mean? Lord, I believe. I want the things that I'm praying about to be mine. I want to walk in your spiritual authority. It doesn't say 'Ask' it says 'Say' so Lord, I speak to these circumstances that I'm facing, and I speak to them believing in Jesus' name."*

Then I read the next verse.

"But when you are praying, first forgive anyone you are holding a grudge against, so that your Father in heaven will forgive your sins, too" (Mark 11:25, NLT).

When I read verse 25, I began to cry. It hit me in the face. *"First forgive anyone you are holding a grudge against..."* I knew that if I wanted to walk in spiritual authority, I first had to walk through the door of forgiveness. I wrote this down in my journal. *"Release others and God will release Himself to you."* I knew this was from the Lord. I knew that if I wanted spiritual authority, I had to forgive. I spent a long time in the presence of God, releasing anyone that I had a grudge against. At the end of that encounter, I was able to say over every person that God brought to my mind, *"No payment required."*

Based off of that one verse, what can you definitively declare about God and forgiveness? Yep, He's attached to it. *"If you want spiritual authority, first forgive..."*

"But, Pastor Matt. You don't know what people have done to me! You don't know how I have been wronged and taken advantage of."

I get it. I've been there, so has God. Think about God and forgiveness. He lives in the realm of forgiveness. He offered His one and only Son on our behalf so that He could extend forgiveness to anyone who believes. Do any of us deserve this? Absolutely not! Does God approve of any of our sinful actions? No, yet He freely offers to anyone the chance to be completely forgiven.

The world's message is just the opposite, and it shouts at us over the top of God's voice. *"Pay them back! Get even! Hold on to it for as long as you can! Don't let them off the hook."*

When we give into the natural inclination of our flesh, holding on to our hurts feels good. It gives us emotion and energy. We play the offense over and over in our minds, how we would pay them back or how we would retaliate now, or how wrong they were for what they did, yet Scripture tells us over and over that we have to forgive.

*"In the same way, you husbands must give honor to your wives. Treat your wife with understanding as you live together. She may be weaker than you are, but she is your equal partner in God's gift of new life. Treat her as you should **so your prayers will not be hindered"*** (1 Peter 3:7, NLT, emphasis mine).

Prayers hindered for not living with your wife in an understanding way? At the most basic level, this should alert you to the attachment of God toward human relationships. God values human relationships. Remember the two greatest commandments according to Jesus? Love God with all your heart..."*and love your neighbor as yourself."*

"Since God chose you to be the holy people he loves, you must clothe yourselves with tenderhearted mercy, kindness, humility, gentleness, and patience. *[13]* *Make allowance for each other's faults, and forgive anyone who offends you. Remember, the Lord forgave you, so you must forgive others.* *[14]* *Above all, clothe yourselves with love, which binds us all together in perfect harmony.* *[15]* *And let the peace that*

comes from Christ rule in your hearts. For as members of one body you are called to live in peace. And always be thankful" (Colossians 3:12-15, NLT).

Pay attention to the language used here. Mercy, kindness, gentleness, patience, allowance for each other's faults, forgiveness, and above all, love. It's all about human interaction. God cares deeply about how we live towards one another. What reason does the Apostle Paul give to the Colossian believers regarding forgiveness? We forgive because God forgave us. This is where God dwells, in the land of forgiveness, and He invites us to live in that place with Him. Notice what Jesus says in Matthew 5.

"So if you are presenting a sacrifice at the altar in the Temple and you suddenly remember that someone has something against you, ²⁴ leave your sacrifice there at the altar. Go and be reconciled to that person. Then come and offer your sacrifice to God" (Matthew 5:23-24, NLT).

Did you catch the order? Reconciliation first, then sacrifice to God. Many of us are offering our sacrifices to God with an offended spirit and we think we are connecting with Him, but we are not, because the offering is out of order. God says to leave the worship, and not offer it until the sacrifice of reconciliation has been offered. It is in this order for a reason because God is attached to forgiveness.

Jesus tells a story to show just how much God is attached to forgiveness. When Peter asks Him how many times he should offer forgiveness, Jesus tells him about a certain servant who owed his king an insurmountable debt. Over 200 million dollars. When the gavel of judgement touched down, the servant begged for forgiveness and mercy, and the king, who was moved with compassion, forgave the entire debt.

On his way home, the servant saw a man who owed him a frivolous amount: a few thousand dollars. The servant flew into a rage and sent the man off to debtor's prison until the full amount could be paid back. News of this reached the king's ear. Notice how Jesus ends the story.

Then the king called in the man he had forgiven and said, 'You evil servant! I forgave you that tremendous debt because you pleaded with me. ³³ Shouldn't you have mercy on your fellow servant, just as I had mercy on you?' ³⁴ Then the angry king sent the man to prison to be tortured until he had paid his entire debt. ³⁵ "That's what my heavenly Father will do to you if you refuse to forgive your brothers and sisters from your heart" (Matthew 18:32-35, NLT).

The servant seemingly forgot about his tremendous debt that was completely forgiven by the gracious king. Are you connecting the dots yet? This is true of us when we lock others way in a prison of unforgiveness. Jesus makes it clear that unforgiveness locks the person withholding it in a prison. The king sent the servant to prison. This is what God does to us, and He has no other choice but to do it. This is how much He is attached to forgiveness. He knows as the wound festers in our lives, it destroys us. He knows that in order for us to be set free, we have to forgive.

However, forgiveness is not natural. It's supernatural, and it's only something God can do in you. When we only operate in the natural realm, forgiveness is an impossible door to open.

C.S. Lewis says that *"Everyone thinks forgiveness is a lovely idea until he has something to forgive."* [1]

That's exactly right.

Maybe you've been hurt by actions.

Maybe someone abused you or sexually assaulted you.

Maybe you were physically beaten. I've counseled with many people who were physically beaten by a drunken parent.

Maybe you've been hurt by emotions.

Maybe a parent told you over and over that you were worthless or will never amount to anything.

Maybe people have attacked you, let you down, mistreated you, and lied about you.

Maybe you've been hurt by words.

Maybe someone ridiculed you, belittled you, or publicly humiliated you.

Maybe you have been betrayed. Your husband was unfaithful to you, or your best friend turned against you.

I have had this happen to me more than once by people I've called *"friends."* If you live with people long enough, eventually they will let you down. Whoever said, *"Sticks and stones will break my bones but words will never hurt me"* was a liar! The Bible says about words that the power of life and death is in the tongue.

Maybe you've been hurt by friends, by parents, by relatives, by your spouse, by church, by God, and you don't know what to do with the hurt and the pain that is so real. Jesus gives some real answers to this very real problem.

Luke 15 is known for the story of the Prodigal Son. Remember him? He cursed his father, wished him dead, destroyed the family name and wasted his life in rebellious living. Everyone in the crowd would have gasped in horror at this young man's despicable actions as Jesus told them the story. But, there is another character at the end of the story that is equally important. Many of you are going to be able to relate to him, because he was dealing with an offended, unforgiving spirit.

Meanwhile, the older son was in the field. When he came near the house, he heard music and dancing. ²⁶ So he called one of the servants and asked him what was going on. ²⁷ "Your brother has come," he replied, "and your father has killed the fattened calf because he has him back safe and sound." ²⁸ "The older brother became angry and refused to go in. So his father went out and pleaded with him. ²⁹ But he answered his father, "Look! All these years I've been slaving for you and never disobeyed your orders. Yet you never gave me even a young goat so I could celebrate with my friends. ³⁰ But when this son of yours who has squandered your property with prostitutes comes home, you kill the fattened calf for him!" ³¹ "My son," the father said, "you are always with me, and everything I have is yours. ³² But we had to celebrate and be glad, because this brother of yours was dead and is alive again; he was lost and is found" (Luke 15:25-32, NIV).

As seen in the older brother, what are the symptoms of an offended spirit?

Anger

"The older brother became angry..." (Luke 15:28a, NIV).

One of the main symptoms of an unforgiving, offended spirit is that you become angry. You experience hurt, and that hurt, if not dealt with, turns to anger. Hurt is the root, anger is the fruit, and you begin to lash out, say hurtful things, think harmful things, and do hateful things. This older brother had anger.

Isolation

"The older brother became angry and refused to go in" (Luke 15:28a/b, NIV).

An offended spirit will often lead to isolation, where a person begins to cut himself or herself off and hide from those who have hurt them. You begin to avoid. You become cold. You shut yourself off, emotionally and physically. The older brother had an offended spirit and refused to go in.

Self-Pity

But he answered his father, "Look! All these years I've been slaving for you and never disobeyed your orders. Yet you never gave me even a young goat so I could celebrate with my friends" (Luke 15:29, NIV).

You know what he was saying? *"I deserve to be treated better than I am. Father, you are unjust and unfair."* Let me point this out: No one who received abuse or betrayal deserved it. It was uncalled for and undeserving.

When I was fired from my church, it hurt. I felt like I didn't deserve to be treated that way, just like you didn't deserve to be treated the way that you did in your situation. This is where the older brother was.

Exaggeration

"But when this son of yours who has squandered your property with prostitutes comes home, you kill the fattened calf for him!" (Luke 15:30, NIV).

Question: How did the older brother know what his younger brother did in the far country? Was he there with him? Was he there when his brother confessed to his father? No! This was an exaggeration that had become a reality in his mind. As the hurt plays over in your mind, it becomes bigger and bigger. The devil makes sure to magnify it to the point that it overtakes your whole life. Have you ever been there?

If left alone and unchecked, what does an unforgiving, offended spirit eventually lead to in your life? Two things:

Barren

*Meanwhile, the older son was in the field. When he came near the house, he heard music and dancing. ²⁶So he called one of the servants and asked him what was going on. "Your brother is back," he was told, "and your father has killed the fattened calf. We are celebrating because of his safe return." ²⁸***The older brother was angry and wouldn't go in** (Luke 15:25-28a, NIV, emphasis mine).

The older brother was in the field working for his father, but he considered himself to be more of a slave than a son. His heart was not right towards his father, just as the younger brother's heart was not right. How do we know this? He came from the field, but he did not go into the house. The text says that he refused to go in where his father and the celebration was.

So, he was not in the field, and he was not in the house. Do you know where he was? He was in limbo, not satisfied in either place. It's called being barren, and that's exactly what happens in a unforgiving heart. No fruit, no blessings, no peace, no fellowship with others and with the Father.

Joyless

"Meanwhile, the older son was in the field. When he came near the house, he heard music and dancing" (Luke 15:25, NIV).

He heard music and dancing, but he was not a part of it. Their joy made him sour. He was angry that they were celebrating and having a good time. Have you ever been there? Someone wronged you and they are now living with a smile on their face and you are not, and it makes you so angry. Unforgiveness robs you of joy. Mark it down. Joy and unforgiveness cannot exist at the same time. The older brother had no joy.

Perhaps even now you recognize that you are living in unforgiveness. What's your next step? What is the solution to an offended spirit? It all revolves around the Father who lives in the land of forgiveness.

The Father's pleading

"The older brother became angry and refused to go in. So his father went out and pleaded with him" (Luke 15:28, NIV).

The older brother refused to draw near to his father, but his father came out to him and pleaded with him. You need to know this about the Lord: He is not willing to leave you with an offended spirit. He is pleading with you to come to Him. To be set free, you must forgive, and

God knows that. God does not want you to stay in that prison of unforgiveness. He wants to heal you.

The Father's presence

"My son," the father said, *"you are always with me..."* (Luke 15:31a, NIV).

The father told the son, *"I'm right here, and I have never left you."* We as believers have that promise as well. Jesus is always with us, and what we desperately need when we've been wounded and hurt is the presence of the Lord. Therefore, we need to take the issue and the wound and the hurt to the Father.

The Bible says to *"Cast your burden on the Lord,"* and to *"Cast your cares on Him, for He cares for you."* He loves it when we run into His presence and make our issues known to Him. He's waiting for you to do that. Some of you need to run into His presence and dwell there and say to the Lord, *"Lord, I refuse to live this way. I'm not leaving until you take this from me."*

The Father's provision

"My son," the father said, *"you are always with me and everything I have is yours"* (Luke 15:31, NIV).

"Everything I have is yours," he said. Don't miss this. Here is what the Lord wants you to know. *"My resources are your resources."* Everything you need in the area of forgiveness and restoration is found in Jesus. Remember, it's supernatural. Forgiveness comes from the supernatural heart of God, and He wants to give that to you.

Paul wrote in the book of Ephesians that *"Every spiritual blessing in the heavenlies belongs to us if we are in Christ Jesus."* Jesus has all the resources you need! The Father had every reason to be offended at the younger son, and yet He acted in a supernatural way. He could have, and should have, disciplined the son who left and the son who refused to come in, but He didn't do that. He responded in the place of God with the response of God, as only God can do.

That same supernatural response is available to us through Jesus. You need to take hold of the Father's provision, and say to the Lord, *"Lord, respond that way in me. Make my heart like your heart. I take hold of Your resources because I have none on my own."*

The interesting thing about the passage is that we don't know how it ends. The father is standing in the field along with the elder son, and that's where Jesus leaves it. I hope that the son embraced the father, walked into the home with him, and forgave his younger brother. That choice now belongs to you.

Will you consider the Father's pleading? He's pleading for you.

Will you consider the Father's presence? He's wanting you to draw near to Him.

Will you consider the Father's provision? He wants to give you His abundant resources to deal with the pain, to deal with the hurt, and to deal with the wounds. I know they are real, but, listen, so is the Father and everything He has for you. The Father is attached to forgiveness. It is only when we walk through the door of forgiveness and allow the Lord to do His supernatural work in us that we obtain spiritual authority. Don't stay barren. Don't stay isolated from Him. Run to him, and be set free in Jesus' name.

Chapter 18

Attached To His Promises

There is a saying in my office that reads *"People are always in a state of discouragement."* For some, it is a great amount. For others, at other times, it may be very minimal. For all of us, at some time or another, discouragement is present, and it is real. I have to remind myself when I preach that there are discouraged people listening to my voice.

What do you do when you are in a state of discouragement? You focus on the promises of God. Do you know that God has promised His children certain things in His Word, and that He is faithful to do what He has promised? Because of that, we can know for sure that God has attached Himself to His promises.

Every time we read the Word of God, we should be looking for those promises. Our prayer life should be transformed as we read those promises, claim those promises, and remind God about what He has promised. There are literally thousands of readily answerable prayers that center on the promises of God, found in His Word. Did you know that? When you read your Bible, you need to underline these verses and pray these back to the Lord. When the Bible says, *"Create in me a clean heart, Oh God,"* do you think that is something God wants to do in your life? Do you think, when you pray that back to Him and ask Him to do that in your heart, do you think He's going to say, *"Nah?"* No! He's going to gladly do it because, once again, He is attached to His Word, and He is attached to prayer. This is so important for you to grasp. The same is true regarding His promises. He wants us to pray these promises back to Him, and He loves it when we do so! Let me show you a great example of how God is attached to His promises. It's found in 2 Corinthians chapter 1.

For Jesus Christ, the Son of God, does not waver between "Yes" and "No." He is the one whom Silas, Timothy, and I preached to you, and as God's ultimate "Yes," he always does what he says. ²⁰ For all of God's promises have been fulfilled in Christ with a resounding "Yes!" And through Christ, our "Amen" (which means "Yes") ascends to God for his glory (2 Corinthians 1:19-20, NIV).

Several things are mentioned in this passage. The first thing you see is that God has made promises. The second thing you see is that He is faithful to these promises by always doing everything He says. Isn't that wonderful? His "*yes*" is always yes and His "*no*" is always no.

Lastly regarding God's promises, all of God's promises have been fulfilled in Christ. Jesus is the resounding "*Amen*" when it comes to God's promises. In other words, Jesus is the means by which the Father can fulfill His promises.

As you read through the Bible, there is one over-arching characteristic of God that always stands out. It is the fact that God, by nature, is a promiser. He loves coming through for His people. He loves showing Himself to be faithful, and He loves for His people to be able to place their complete confidence in Him. Notice how Peter describes the promise keeping God.

"And because of his glory and excellence, he has given us great and precious promises. These are the promises that enable you to share his divine nature and escape the world's corruption caused by human desires" (1 Peter 1:4, NLT).

What does Peter call these promises? Great and precious promises, because He knows that God is a promise keeping God, and that God is attached to His promises. They are precious because they are true.

But, if He's attached to His promises, and all of those promises have been fulfilled in the Lord Jesus Christ, what exactly has Jesus secured for us who know Him and trust in Him? What exactly are these promises that are guaranteed for us through Jesus? Let's rejoice in the following!

The Promise to Save Us

The plan to save humanity was put into motion long before the world was ever created.

"And all the people who belong to this world worshiped the beast. They are the ones whose names were not written in the Book of Life that belongs to the Lamb who was slaughtered before the world was made" (Revelation 13:8, NLT).

God knew that Adam and Eve would rebel in the Garden. He knew that sin would separate mankind from Himself. The sacrificial system in the Old Testament was just a picture, just a glimpse of His redemption, that always pointed to something else, something greater. Jesus was not plan B, He has always been plan A. The High Priest in the Old Testament had no power to take away sin. He was sinful, representing a sinful people. But what does the book of Hebrews say about Jesus?

"Even though Jesus was God's Son, he learned obedience from the things he suffered. 9 In this way, God qualified him as a perfect High Priest, and he became the source of eternal salvation for all those who obey him" (Hebrews 5:8-9, NLT).

Jesus is the perfect High Priest. Jesus is the source of eternal salvation. The cross is where His blood was poured out. It was not with the blood of goats or calves by which we were redeemed, but with the precious blood of Christ. The perfectly innocent took the place of the thoroughly guilty. He washed away our sins, and He instead gave us His perfect righteousness. He said these words on the cross, *"It is finished,"* and it was the resurrection that secured that statement forever.

There is no more need for atonement. Jesus provided everything we need.

There is no more need for a mediator. Jesus is the great Mediator.

There is no more need for a priest. Jesus is our great High Priest.

There is no more need to work for our salvation. Jesus paid it all!

God has promised us salvation that has been secured forever by Jesus for those who place their trust in Him.

The Promise to Be Personal to Us

When the Lord comes in, He doesn't come in as a drill sergeant, barking out orders like an overbearing parent. Instead, He promises to be personal to us who believe. What was it like in the Garden of Eden before Adam and Eve sinned? The Bible says that the Lord walked in the Garden with them in the cool of the day. But, when they sinned, that broke the fellowship that they had with the Lord. Jesus restored that promise by His completed work on the cross, for everyone who believes. What does Jesus now call us who believe? Friends!

"I no longer call you servants, because a servant does not know his master's business. Instead, I have called you friends, for everything that I learned from my Father I have made known to you" (John 15:15, NIV).

Jesus has made us His friends which lets us know that He opens the door of fellowship to us and that He deeply cares about you and me.

"Give all your worries and cares to God, for he cares about you" (1 Peter 5:7, NLT).

Think about that! God cares about you and me. That means that He cares about our suffering, our pain, our rejoicing, our victories just as an attentive parent cares about the details of his or her son or daughter's world. God is personal to us and He cares.

How else is He personal to us? God promises that He will supply our every need.

"And this same God who takes care of me will supply all your needs from his glorious riches, which have been given to us in Christ Jesus" (Philippians 4:19, NLT).

Did God take care of the nation of Israel even when they were living in outright disobedience to Him? Did God take care of the Apostle Paul as he traveled around preaching the Gospel? Paul said that God has taken care of his every need, and he knows, without a doubt, that God will also supply our every need. He is personal to us in every way. This is a promise from God that we can always count on.

The Promise to Privilege Us

Not only is there the promise to be personal, but there is also the promise from God to privilege those who trust in Him. The understanding of privilege didn't click with me until after I was fired from my pastorate, and I was invited to the gym by a friend. He took me to *Planet Fitness* using his Black Card. We went up to the counter, and he said to the person behind the counter, *"He's with me."* I was checked in and didn't have to pay, no questions asked. After we exercised, he then asked me if I wanted to try out the massage chair.

I said, *"Can I do that?"*

He said, *"I've got a black card. You can go anywhere I go."*

Then it dawned on me. Jesus has a black card! Think about it.

*"Therefore if any man be **in Christ**, he is a new creature"* (2 Corinthians 5:17, KJV, emphasis mine).

"In Christ" means that we are in Him. Wherever He goes, we go. Whatever privileges He has, we have. Think about this using the illustration

of a book. If I hide an object in a book and give the book to you, what happens to the object in the book? It goes to you. If the book burns, what happens to the object in the book? It burns, too. Like an object in a book, whatever happens to Jesus happens to you because if Christ is living within you, you are living within Him. This is the privilege that I'm talking about! This means:

How ever God feels about Jesus, He feels about you!

Whatever access Jesus has, you have!

Is Jesus accepted by the Father? Of course!

Is Jesus no longer guilty? Of course!

Does Jesus have full access to the Father? Of course!

Is the Father ever going to cast Jesus away? There's no way!

Is Jesus fully righteous? Of course!

Does Jesus have eternal life? Yes, Yes, Yes!

Is Jesus loved by God? Absolutely! How much is Jesus loved by the Father?

You say, *"Jesus is extremely loved by the Father. It cannot be described or measured."* Would you agree with that? Make the connection! If you are IN CHRIST, doesn't He love you in the exact same way? If you fully understand that you are IN CHRIST, never again do you ever have to wonder, does God love me?

Never again do you have to wonder if you have access to God. Never again do you have to wonder if you have privilege before God. Because of the promise of Jesus, you have undeserved privilege, and because of that, this means that the crescendo of that privilege will be realized in Jesus coming back for us so that we can be with the Father forever and ever. That's a promise you can count on! Jesus is coming again!

What then do you do with all of these promises that are found in the Word of God? What do you do with them? Yes, you have to believe them, but also, you have to remind God often about them. *"Remind God?"* Absolutely!

There are going to be moments in your life when you look at your bank account and you read in God's Word that He will not let the godly go hungry, and you are going to have to remind God of that fact. There's going to be moments in your life when your back is against the wall with no way of escape. This is the moment in your prayer life when urgency calls upon you to throw God's promises back into His face. Many times it will be the only thing you have to lay hold of. Let me show you Biblically what I'm talking about.

Remember King Jehoshaphat? We briefly touched his story found in 2 Chronicles 20 a few chapters earlier. He's the king who had three armies bearing down on him and the nation of Judah. They literally were camped a few miles outside of town.

Instead of scheming and figuring how to handle the situation in his own power using his own resources, he instead begs the Lord for guidance. This is his first inclination upon hearing the imminent news, not his last resort. He then commands everyone in Judah to begin fasting and praying. Again, these are things to which God has attached Himself. Jehoshaphat knew that if God didn't come through for them, they were sunk.

What I want to do is analyze his prayer for you because in his prayer of desperation before the Lord, he takes it upon himself to remind God of all His promises to His people. Before we look at this prayer, I want us to take note of one thing.

"Jehoshaphat stood before the community of Judah and Jerusalem in front of the new courtyard at the Temple of the LORD. He prayed..." (2 Chronicles 20:5-6a NLT).

Jehoshaphat's prayer to remind God was not done in private behind closed doors. He publicly calls God out on His promises. This is bold. This is not quiet and reverent. He involves the entire nation of Judah in his prayer to confront and remind the Lord about what He has promised. Isn't that great? What exactly did he say to the Lord in front of all the people?

He reminds God of His power

He prayed, "O LORD, God of our ancestors, you alone are the God who is in heaven. You are ruler of all the kingdoms of the earth. You are powerful and mighty; no one can stand against you!" (2 Chronicles 20:6, NLT).

"God, there is no one like You, no one that can stand against You." When he did that, Jehoshaphat reminded himself of the kind of God he served, and He reminded God of the kind of God He is! He is the Lord of Heaven, the Lord of Heaven's armies, who rules over all the kingdoms of the earth, all wise, all knowing and all powerful. This is the first thing you do when you begin praying to the Lord. The enemy would like nothing more than for you to forget about the power of God, but the God we serve is a God who is able to do amazing things.

He reminds God of His plan

"O our God, did you not drive out those who lived in this land when your people Israel arrived? And did you not give this land forever to the descendants of your friend Abraham?" (2 Chronicles 20:7, NLT).

"Hey God, You gave this land forever to Your friend Abraham and to all his friends. Remember that? This is Your idea to put us here." In other words, he reminds God that all of this belongs on His shoulders, not theirs. This is His problem, not theirs, and God's shoulders are big enough to carry our biggest problems.

He reminds God of His promises

"Your people settled here and built this Temple to honor your name. ⁹ They said, 'Whenever we are faced with any calamity such as war,

plague, or famine, we can come to stand in your presence before this Temple where your name is honored. We can cry out to you to save us, and you will hear us and rescue us" (2 Chronicles 20:8-9, NLT).

This is what King Solomon prayed when the Temple was dedicated to the Lord. King Jehoshaphat took it upon himself to remind God about what was said and what was promised. *"We can cry out to You to save us, and you will hear and rescue us."* Don't miss the spiritual lesson here. It is okay to remind God of what He has promised in His Word. Sometimes, it's the only thing you have to hold on to.

He reminds God of His perception

"And now see what the armies of Ammon, Moab, and Mount Seir are doing. You would not let our ancestors invade those nations when Israel left Egypt, so they went around them and did not destroy them. [11] *Now see how they reward us! For they have come to throw us out of your land, which you gave us as an inheritance"* (2 Chronicles 20:10-11, NLT).

"God, do you see what they are doing? Do you see what is going on?" Listen, it is okay to tell God what is going on in your life. It is okay to pour out your heart to God and passionately plead your case to God. Does He already know what's going on? Yes, but we have to start praying as if He doesn't.

A hospice chaplain told a story about a man in the last stages of cancer. The man felt guilty and horrible because he spent the night before ranting and raving and swearing, telling God everything that was on his mind. The chaplain asked *"Do you know the Christian word that describes what you have been doing? The word is 'prayer.' You have spent the night praying."* [1]

Sojourner Truth, the ex-slave who was a leader in the abolition of slavery and the woman's suffrage movement, knew how to pray like Jehoshaphat. Once she labored in prayer for her missing son. This is what she prayed:

"Oh, God, you know how much I am distressed, for I have told you again and again. Now, God, help me get my son. If you were in trouble, as I am, and I could help you, as you can me, think I wouldn't do it? Yes, God you know I would do it." [2]

Once when she was having a hard time financially, she prayed this:

"O God, you know I have no money, but you can make the people do for me, and must make the people do for me. I will never give you peace till you do God." [3]

Martin Luther, the great Reformer, says this of reminding God about His promises as he prayed fervently for the wellness of his fellow Reformer, Phillip Melanchthon.

"Our Lord could not but hear me; I threw the sack down before his door. I rubbed God's ear with all his promises about hearing prayer. I besought the Almighty with great vigor. I attacked him with his own weapons, quoting from Scripture all the promises that I could remember and said that he must grant my prayer if I was henceforth to put faith in his promises." [4]

Pastor Tony Evans tells a story about Pastors who were gathering for a city-wide crusade meeting in South Carolina. The weather forecast called for heavy rain that would more than likely cancel the event. They decided to pray something like this: *"Lord, if it be Your will"* and *"Lord, help us not to get too wet."* Then a little bitty woman named Linda, in the midst of all these Pastors, started to pray.

"Lord, Your name is at stake. We told these people that if they come, they would hear a word from God. If they come, and You let it rain, and You control the weather, then You look bad because we told them that You wanted to say something to them. So, if we told them that You wanted to say something to them, and You don't keep back what You can control so it can be said to them, then Your name is bad. Therefore, right now, I command You in the name of the Lord Jesus Christ to stop the rain for the sake of Your Name."

Tony Evans said that the Pastors kind of one-eyed each other when she got to that part about commanding God. As they were sitting on the platform at 7pm, dark skies and thunder and lightning were all around them. One of the Pastors pulled out an umbrella and tried to cover Linda with it, but she pushed it back and said, *"I don't need it."* Then it happened. Pastor Evans said that as the storm approached the stadium, the storm actually parted and went around the stadium and then came back together on the other side. 4

This prayerful woman told God what was going on and demanded that He act, and God listened! Understand that is okay to emphatically and passionately remind God and let Him know what is going on in your situation.

He reminds God of His passion

"O our God, won't you stop them? We are powerless against this mighty army that is about to attack us. We do not know what to do, but we are looking to you for help" (2 Chronicles 20:12, NLT).

"God, we are passionately looking to You for help. Be passionate about us." This is what Jehoshaphat prays to God. *"We don't know what to do, respond with passion to our problem."* Do you know what the Bible says about God? It says that He is passionate for His people, and that He loves to come to the rescue. Remind Him of His promised passion!

How does the story end? God shows up in a mighty way and saves His people. When we are faced with a difficult circumstance, we must remember the promises of God. He's attached to them.

We also must remind God of them often. We must remind Him of them passionately and publicly in the company of other believers. We must call upon God as if our very lives depend on it, just like tiny Linda did. He's not threatened by us holding Him to His promises. He loves to be put on the spot, come through for His children, and be faithful to what He has promised and be faithful to what He is attached.

[1] Phillip Yancey, "Prayer: Does It Make Any Difference?" (Unabridged Edition, Zondervan, 2006), 10.

[2] Sojourner Truth, *The Narrative of Sojourner Truth;* edited by Olive Gilbert; Appendix by Theodore D. Weld, (J. B. Yerrington and Son, Boston, 1850), 59. www.digital.library.upenn.edu.

[3] Ibid.

[4] Phillip Yancey, "Prayer: Does It Make Any Difference?" (Unabridged Edition, Zondervan, 2006), 94.

[5] Tony Evans, *The Storm,* (The Urban Alternative, 2011). www.tonyevans.org. www.youtube.com/watch?v=zE7YomvT2eo.

Chapter 19

Attached To His Name

The book of Proverbs says that a good name is better than great riches. Did your mom ever tell you that? I know Truett Cathy's mom more than likely did because that verse is the foundational verse of the Chick-fil-A philosophy of business. Everything they do as a company is centered around their name; how they relate to a customer, how they serve the food, how quickly they serve the food, the quality of their food, the commitment to their employees, and their charitable giving. Everything to them in business revolves around having a good name and a good reputation.

Think about a professional ball club. What happens when the player's name on the back of the jersey brings shame to the franchise name on the front of the jersey? The name on the back of the jersey is often removed. I've reminded my kids of this many times, and they have seen this come to fruition in the lives of many professional athletes.

How does your family feel about their name? Did your parents ever talk with you about remembering to keep the family name in good standing as you went on a date or out with the guys? Why did they do that? Because their name and their reputation is important to them. They do not want any shame to be brought to the family name.

A good name means a lot, and most people care about the standing of their good name. For instance: has anyone ever told lies about you?

How did you feel when that happened? Has anyone ever put words in your mouth that you did not say? How did you react? Has anyone ever attributed something to you that you didn't do? How did that make you feel? The reason we get upset when our name is misused is that we care about our reputation. Isn't that right?

God feels the same way about His name. If you read through the pages of Scripture, you will constantly see just how much God cares and acts because of His name. He cares how His name is revered, and He cares how it is viewed, but why? Why does He care so much about His name? He cares so much because He's attached to it. His character and reputation and everything that He is, is wrapped up in His name. In other words, when you speak the name of God, you are speaking about all that He is and nothing that He is not. For instance:

His greatness is bound to His name

"Our ancestors in Egypt were not impressed by the LORD's miraculous deeds. They soon forgot his many acts of kindness to them. Instead, they rebelled against him at the Red Sea. ⁸ Even so, he saved them— to defend the honor of his name and to demonstrate his mighty power" (Psalm 106:7-8, NLT).

Why did He choose to rescue rebellious Israel? He did it to defend His name and to demonstrate His mighty power.

His faithfulness is bound to His name

"The LORD will not abandon his people, because that would dishonor his great name. For it has pleased the LORD to make you his very own people" (1 Samuel 12:22, NLT).

When the people came to Samuel asking for a human, earthly king to rule over them, the Lord took it as a personal matter. He tells Samuel that they have rejected not him but I, the Lord. What does the Lord say to the thought His people turning away from Him in worship of other gods? *"I will not abandon you and bring dishonor to my great name."*

He says this because He is faithful, even when we are woefully unfaithful.

His mercy is bound to His name

"Help us, O God of our salvation! Help us for the glory of your name. Save us and forgive our sins for the honor of your name" (Psalm 79:9, NLT).

When Jerusalem was under siege, the Psalmist appealed to the mercy of God which is bound to His name.

His goodness is bound to His name

"When the queen of Sheba heard of Solomon's fame, which brought honor to the name of the LORD, she came to test him with hard questions" (1 Kings 10:1, NLT).

The Queen of Sheba heard about Solomon's fame and came to him to check it out for herself. When she had thoroughly tested him in every way, she exclaims in verse 9:

"Praise the LORD your God, who delights in you and has placed you on the throne of Israel. Because of the LORD's eternal love for Israel, he has made you king so you can rule with justice and righteousness" (1 Kings 10:9, NLT).

She gave glory to the Lord because of the goodness and blessings of God towards Solomon! This is why God honored Solomon so that He, God, could receive honor and glory through his life.

Now can you clearly see the attachment of God to His name? This is why it says in Exodus 20:7, *"You shall not misuse the name of the Lord your God, for the Lord will not hold anyone guiltless who misuses His name" (NIV).* He issues this judgement because everything that God is, is wrapped up in His name.

Remember what happened in Exodus 32? Moses went into the mountains to commune with God and receive the 10 Commandments. What did the people do when he didn't immediately return? They began feasting and dancing and glorifying a golden calf as the true *"god"* that led them out of Egypt. Notice what God suggests to do as a result of this rebellion.

Then the Lord said, "I have seen how stubborn and rebellious these people are. ¹⁰ Now leave me alone so my fierce anger can blaze against them, and I will destroy them. Then I will make you, Moses, into a great nation."

¹¹ But Moses tried to pacify the Lord his God. "O Lord!" he said. "Why are you so angry with your own people whom you brought from the land of Egypt with such great power and such a strong hand? ¹² Why let the Egyptians say, 'Their God rescued them with the evil intention of slaughtering them in the mountains and wiping them from the face of the earth'? Turn away from your fierce anger. Change your mind about this terrible disaster you have threatened against your people! ¹³ Remember your servants Abraham, Isaac, and Jacob. You bound yourself with an oath to them, saying, 'I will make your descendants as numerous as the stars of heaven. And I will give them all of this land that I have promised to your descendants, and they will possess it forever.'"

¹⁴ So the Lord changed his mind about the terrible disaster he had threatened to bring on his people. (Exodus 32:9-14, NLT).

God says, *"Step aside, Moses. I'm about to start everything over and begin again with you."* Did you read what Moses says to God? He appeals to His reputation. *"Why let the Egyptians say…"* In other words, *"God, if you do this, you are going to be the laughing stock of the Egyptians."*

He also appeals to His promises. *"Remember your servants Abraham, Isaac, and Jacob." "Lord, don't forget that You already promised an oath to Abraham."*

Moses knows that God is attached to what He has said. How does the discourse end? *"So the Lord changed His mind..."* because Moses reminded Him about His reputation, His promises, and ultimately about His name.

Reputation and promise. These are two foundational themes surrounding God's name. He acts according to what He has promised, and He acts according to His reputation because He's attached to His name.

Notice how others in the Bible appealed to the reputation and promise of God according to His name.

*"O my God, lean down and listen to me. Open your eyes and see our despair. See how your city—**the city that bears your name**—lies in ruins. We make this plea, not because we deserve help, but because of your mercy. ¹⁹ O Lord, hear. O Lord, forgive. O Lord, listen and act! For your own sake, do not delay, O my God, **for your people and your city bear your name**"* (Daniel 9:18-19, NLT, emphasis mine).

Daniel says, *"God, You have to help us because we are living in a city that bears your name, and we are a people that bear Your name."* Daniel understood the reputation of God and knew that God is attached to His name.

In Ezekiel 20, God recounts for His people how they have constantly rebelled against Him. In each and every moment that He thinks about destroying them, He stops. Why? Look at how many times in the passage He acts according to His promise and His reputation.

*"But I didn't do it, **for I acted to protect the honor of my name. I would not allow shame to be brought on my name** among the surrounding nations who saw me reveal myself by bringing the Israelites out of Egypt"* (Ezekiel 20:9, NLT, emphasis mine).

*"But again I held back in order **to protect the honor of my name** before the nations who had seen my power in bringing Israel out of Egypt"* (Ezekiel 20:14, NLT, emphasis mine).

*"Nevertheless, I withdrew my judgment against them **to protect the honor of my name** before the nations that had seen my power in bringing them out of Egypt"* (Ezekiel 20:22, NLT, emphasis mine).

*"As for you, O people of Israel, this is what the Sovereign LORD says: Go right ahead and worship your idols, but sooner or later you will obey me and will **stop bringing shame on my holy name** by worshiping idols"* (Ezekiel 20:39, NLT, emphasis mine).

*"You will know that I am the LORD, O people of Israel, **when I have honored my name** by treating you mercifully in spite of your wickedness. I, the Sovereign LORD, have spoken!"* (Ezekiel 20:44, NLT, emphasis mine).

Do you see just how much God cares about His reputation and His promises according to His name? There are so many more passages in the Bible that clearly show that God is attached to His name. The question that we have to answer regarding this is, why? Why does God act and respond according to His name? Why does God care so much about His name? Look at what Paul tells the Church in Rome in the beginning of his letter to them.

*"Through Christ, God has given us the privilege and authority as apostles to tell Gentiles everywhere what God has done for them, so that they will believe and obey him, **bringing glory to his name"*** (Romans 1:5, NLT, emphasis mine.)

Why does Paul make it his mission to tell Gentiles the glorious news of the Gospel? It is so that they can believe and obey the Lord, bringing glory to His name.

This is the culmination of our response to God. He wants all glory to be brought to His name. Look at what the Son says to the Father and the Father says to the Son in John chapter 12.

"Now my soul is deeply troubled. Should I pray, 'Father, save me from this hour'? But this is the very reason I came! Father, bring glory to your name."

Then a voice spoke from heaven, saying, "I have already brought glory to my name, and I will do so again" (John 12:27-28, NLT)

Jesus, speaking about His death, pleaded for glory to be brought to the Father's name, and the Father answered Him saying, *"I have already brought glory to my name, and I will do so again."*

What does *"glory"* mean when it pertains to God? It means that He wants all eyes on Him. He wants the focus of everyone on earth to be squarely on Him. He wants all worship to be given only to Him. He wants every voice lifted in praise to Him so that He can be fully and completely glorified!

This is why it matters what we do or don't do as God's children, called by His name. Either we glorify the name of God or we dishonor it. When we dishonor it, we are actually producing a false picture of God, distorting His true image and character, bringing shame to His person.

God has concern for how His name is represented among the peoples of the earth. When ancient Israel dishonored His name, God scattered them among the nations. When they continued to profane the name of the Lord in front of their captors, the Lord brought them back home. Why?

But when they were scattered among the nations, they brought shame on my holy name. For the nations said, "These are the people of the LORD, but he couldn't keep them safe in his own land!" [21] *Then I was concerned for my holy name, on which my people brought shame among the nations.* [22] *"Therefore, give the people of Israel this message from the Sovereign LORD: I am bringing you back, but not because you deserve it. I am doing it to protect my holy name, on which you brought shame while you were scattered among the nations"* (Ezekiel 36:20-22, NLT).

He brought them back, not because they deserved it, but only to preserve and protect and uphold His reputation and good name! This is why the Apostle Paul says for us:

"Whether you eat or drink, or whatever you do, do all to the glory of God" (1 Corinthians 10:31, NIV).

In other words, nothing is mundane when it comes to the glory of God! Even our eating and drinking should bring Him the utmost glory.

I want us to think further about this idea of God receiving glory and the great lengths to which God goes to get it. If you remember in the pages of Scripture, Jesus often healed physical bodies. As a matter of fact, it was His healing power that authenticated His saving power to forgive sins.

In John 9, Jesus heals a man born blind. Jesus makes mud, spreads it over the man's eyes and tells him to wash in the pool of Siloam. When the man came back from washing, he could miraculously see. The miracle caused quite an uproar if you read the passage. People were actually convinced that the man born blind was someone else! This couldn't have been the man that they had always known because this man could see!

When the religious leaders got involved in the questioning, they demanded to know who healed him, but he didn't know. He just knew that the man who performed the miracle had to be someone special. Look at what he tells the religious people.

"Ever since the world began, no one has been able to open the eyes of someone born blind. 33 If this man were not from God, he couldn't have done it" (John 9:32-33).

Why did he say that? It is because only God can open the eyes of the blind, and only God should receive all glory. In Mark 1, Jesus does something else that only God could do.

A man with leprosy came and knelt in front of Jesus, begging to be healed. "If you are willing, you can heal me and make me clean," he said. ⁴¹ Moved with compassion, Jesus reached out and touched him. "I am willing," he said. "Be healed!" ⁴² Instantly the leprosy disappeared, and the man was healed (Mark 1:40-42, NLT).

Again, leprosy was such a disease that there was no hope of ever getting rid of it apart from divine intervention. In this situation, God intervened and the man was instantly healed. Glory was given to God because only God has the power to miraculously heal.

Remember the story of Lazarus in John 11? Jesus intentionally stayed away for two additional days when He heard that His friend had died. Why? It was so that He could show the disciples that He has authority, even over death. Look at John 11:

Then Jesus shouted, "Lazarus, come out!" ⁴⁴ And the dead man came out, his hands and feet bound in graveclothes, his face wrapped in a headcloth. Jesus told them, "Unwrap him and let him go!" (John 11:43-44).

Once again, the attention of everyone was on God, and glory was given to Him because only God has the power to raise the dead.

In chapter 10 of the Book of Joshua, it says that soon after Joshua and the Israelites entered the Promised Land, they waged battle against five armies. Joshua prayed and asked God help the Israelites in their battle by stopping the sun:

On the day the Lord gave the Israelites victory over the Amorites, Joshua prayed to the Lord in front of all the people of Israel. He said, "Let the sun stand still over Gibeon, and the moon over the valley of Aijalon." ¹³ So the sun stood still and the moon stayed in place until the nation of Israel had defeated its enemies. Is this event not recorded in The Book of Jashar? The sun stayed in the middle of the sky, and it did not set as on a normal day. ¹⁴ There has never been a day like this one before or since, when the Lord answered such a prayer. Surely the Lord fought for Israel that day! (Joshua 10:12-14, NLT).

When Amy and I were in Israel, we got to fly over Israel in a helicopter, accompanied by an archeologist named Thomas. While we were in the air, Thomas said to us, *"See that hillside down there? That's the place where Joshua asked God to make the sun stand still."* And we were like *"Wooowww."* God brought Himself glory by bending the laws of nature, because again, that's only something God can do.

Stop and reflect for one minute about what we see and behold in nature. It all is evidence of God, and it all points to the glory of God. The sky, the stars, the skin on your body, your hair, the sun, the flowers in the field, the birds in the trees, everything that is in nature came about by the creativity of God, and for that God should receive praise and glory! Isn't that right? But how did God choose to bring everything into existence?

Ex nihilo

One way is called in the Latin *"Ex nihilo"* which means, *"from nothing."* It refers to God creating everything from nothing. Prior to Genesis 1:1 there was nothing. God didn't make the universe from preexisting building blocks. He started from scratch. The Biblical testimony insists that in the beginning, there was nothing apart from God, and what exists was brought into being by Him. Look at Hebrews 11:

"By faith we understand that the entire universe was formed at God's command, that what we now see did not come from anything that can be seen" (Hebrews 11:3, NLT).

Do you know that evolution is predicated on the fact that everything builds upon itself? This turns into this and this turns into this, but Hebrews 11 clearly says that *"what we now see did not come from anything that can be seen."* This is ex-nihilo, *"creation of everything from nothing."* But, how did He bring things into existence?

With His Voice

Let me give you some verses that clearly show this.

In Mark 4, when a life-threatening storm came upon Jesus and His disciples, how did Jesus calm the storm? He calmed it by only using His voice.

When Jesus woke up, he rebuked the wind and said to the waves, "Silence! Be still!" Suddenly the wind stopped, and there was a great calm (Mark 4:39, NLT).

He rebuked the wind and spoke to the waves. Remember Jesus raising Lazarus from the dead in John 11? How did He raise Lazarus? He spoke to Him. He used His voice to summon Lazarus from the dead. Only God can do this! Look at what the Psalmist says about the voice of the Lord:

"The Lord merely spoke, and the heavens were created. He breathed the word, and all the stars were born. ⁷ He assigned the sea its boundaries and locked the oceans in vast reservoirs. ⁸ Let the whole world fear the Lord, and let everyone stand in awe of him. ⁹ For when he spoke, the world began! It appeared at his command" (Psalm 33:6-9, NLT).

Notice what Peter says about this:

"They deliberately forget that God made the heavens long ago by the word of his command, and he brought the earth out from the water and surrounded it with water" (2 Peter 3:5, NLT).

Peter tells his audience and these scoffers that God made the heavens by the word of His command. The Psalmist says that He breathed and all the stars were born! This is something that only God can do, and only God is responsible for everything we see!

Let's dig a little deeper into this. Numbers 20 has always puzzled me. God tells Moses to speak to the rock to allow water to come out, but instead, Moses hits the rock and water flows out. For hitting the rock and not speaking to it, God tells Moses that he will not be allowed to enter the Promised Land. Why? It seems like such a little thing, until you understand why God wanted Him to speak.

Moses was standing in the place of God before the people. God tells him to speak to the rock and make the water flow to demonstrate that only God can call for things to happen by His spoken word alone. Instead of demonstrating the power of God's spoken word, Moses instead hits the rock in His own power. He in essence, steals the show from God and puts the spotlight on himself. If Moses would have spoken to the rock, everyone would have known that God did it, and that God was among them because it's only something that God can do. Instead, Moses acted in his own power and took glory away from the Lord. What does God think about glory being taken away from Him? Look at Isaiah 48:

"For my own sake, for my own sake, I do this. How can I let myself be defamed? **I will not yield my glory to another***"* (Isaiah 48:11, NIV, emphasis mine).

Moses did something that no one should ever do. He forgot that God goes to great lengths, as I've just shown you, to display His glory, and He never shares His glory with anyone. Moses learned, as should we, that when you steal glory from God, you pay the price. God wants every eye to be fully focused on Him. This is why He keeps His promises. This is why He acts. This is why He fiercely upholds His reputation. This is why He does great things. It is all because He is attached to His name, and He wants all glory to be brought to it.

What should this cause us to do?

The God we serve is a great God! He has promised to do certain things, and his reputation is on the line! He is not a liar. He is not unfaithful. He is a promise keeping God! Therefore,

Appeal

If He's attached to His name, appeal to it! If He has made promises, hold Him to that! As I have mentioned before, turn your Bible study time into a time of appeal. Put back on Him everything that He has promised in the Word of God. Lay those promises out before Him and hold Him to those. He is faithful, and He loves coming through for His people!

Appeal to His goodness. Appeal to His mercy. Appeal to His power. He is the Creator of the Heavens and the earth, and He has the ability to move both of those out of the way on our behalf, for His glory. Only He has the power to turn around seemingly-impossible situations, and only He has the power to raise the dead, speak things into existence, create from nothing, bend the laws of nature, and on and on we could go. He's attached to His name. Therefore, appeal to it!

Glorify

Yes, you should appeal to His name, and you should also do everything in your power to bring glory to His name in every circumstance and in every moment of existence, even when life seems menial and mundane. When you eat, glorify God. When you walk, glorify God. When you speak, glorify God. When you study, glorify God. When He rescues, comes through and saves, the spotlight is fully on Him. Keep it on Him! This is His glory. He is center stage, and He stands ready to bask in the praises of His creation.

When we live for His glory, it means that the glory of His person shines brightly in and through us. Therefore, live in such a way that it brings to God the most glory.

Living for His glory also means that we will automatically live in the place of blessing. When we glorify God, we are blessed, and we are doing that for which we have been created. As we appeal to His name and bring glory to His name, the Father will receive praise, and we will dwell in the good presence of our great and awesome God!

He's attached to His name. Therefore, appeal to it and bring glory to it as a watching world watches you. And, as they watch you, reflect their eyes off of you and on to Him, to whom all glory belongs. Amen!

The purpose of this book is to be a guide for you as you celebrate the 7 feasts as a New Testament family. In each section you will find a brief overview about each feast and a step-by-step guide on how you can tangibly celebrate that particular feast.

By choosing to creatively celebrate these feasts as a family, you will be giving your children a valuable gift-the gift of Scripture. Not only will they hear the salvation story of God year after year in an exciting, fun and creative way, they will know that story by heart. This book is designed to be a real discipleship tool that you can use to teach your children. As you celebrate these feasts as a family year after year, your children will begin to know the Bible from front to back and they will know the beautiful story of redemption that God has woven so gracefully throughout the pages of Scripture.

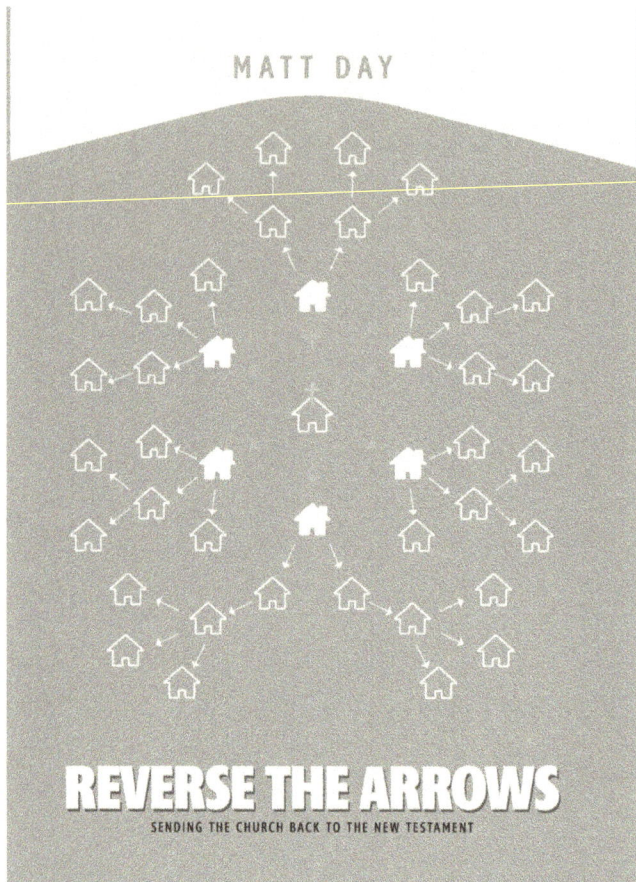

MATT DAY

REVERSE THE ARROWS

SENDING THE CHURCH BACK TO THE NEW TESTAMENT

DOES THE CHURCH TODAY LOOK LIKE THE NEW TESTAMENT CHURCH?

The Church in the U.S. in rapid decline? Believers not maturing? Some Pastors believing that "cultural Christians" are filling up their churches?

What can be done about this? Do we go back in safety to what we've always known, or do we begin thinking differently, thinking Biblically?

What if we courageously began thinking differently? What if COVID-19 is God's way of forcing us to think differently as we reverse the arrows?

Instead of having the arrows point into the church building, we could reverse the arrows and resource God's people to turn houses, coffee shops, schools, offices, huts into churches and enable them to be the local church right where they are, just like they did in the New Testament!

The New Testament Church is a "micro" movement. Because of intense persecution throughout the Roman Empire, the church grew from "house to house." This is the context of the New Testament Church. It is a movement focused on reversing the arrows away from the Church sitting to the Church going and expanding the Kingdom.

Throughout this book, Pastor Matt Day gives compelling statistical evidence and Biblical evidence as to why the arrows must be reversed in the Church, and he gives you the resources needed to do just that. This is a must read for every Pastor and every church body.

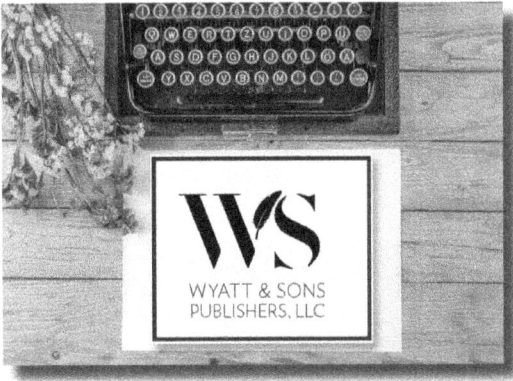

You have a story.
We want to publish it.

Everyone has as a story to tell. It might be about something you know how to do, or what has happened in your life, or it may be a thrilling, or romantic, or intriguing, or heartwarming, or suspenseful story, starring a cast of characters that have been swimming around in your imagination.

And at Wyatt & Sons Publishers, we can get your story onto the pages of a book just like the one you are holding in your hand. With professional interior design and a custom, professionally designed cover built just for you from the start, you can finally see your dream of being an author become reality. Then, you will see your book listed with retailers all over the world as people are able to buy your book from wherever they are and have it delivered to their home or their e-reader.

So what are you waiting for? This is your time.

visit us at

www.wyattpublishing.com

for details on how to get started becoming a
published author right away.

www.ingramcontent.com/pod-product-compliance
Lightning Source LLC
Chambersburg PA
CBHW030506100426
42813CB00002B/362